TH

Photogr

Guide

TO

NORTHUMBERLAND

www.longvalleybooks.com

ISBN: 978 0 9926834 50

Published by Long Valley Books Ltd.

With thanks to Jane Ellingham for her help with proofreading and Neil Berry for his never ending support. I'd also like to thank all the photographers who have allowed me to use their stunning photos (see page 121 for details).

Printed by MTP Media Ltd, Kendal.

Contents

SECTION 1 » The Coast Part 1 – Berwick to Holy Island

SECTION 2 » The Coast Part 2 – Bamburgh to Alnmouth

SECTION 3 » The Coast Part 3 – Amble to Tynemouth

SECTION 4 » Castles & Countryside

SECTION 5» Hadrian's Wall

Introduction

The stunning Northumberland coast has some of the finest photography locations in the UK, with romantic castles, miles of glorious golden beaches, elegant grass-covered dunes and dramatic shoreline geology. This irresistible mix creates a wealth of potential for seascapes and inner landscapes alike. It's an outstanding area to explore, but you'll find there's even more to Northumberland if you venture inland. The countryside has various hidden gems, from secret waterfalls and ancient monuments to marvellous heather moorlands, as well as more magnificent castles. And last, but by no means least, there's Hadrian's Wall – an impressive feat of Roman engineering with many atmospheric and photogenic locations along its length.

Whether you're totally unfamiliar with Northumberland or you've spent some time there already, this guide will help you to choose where to photograph, when to go for the best conditions, and most importantly how to actually get there. It doesn't matter whether you're a beginner with a compact camera just starting out, or a seasoned photographer with all the kit — it's still just about getting out in the landscape and enjoying capturing these beautiful places.

For each location I've given the most direct way to get there, and many locations can be combined together in a day trip. When you arrive at your chosen location I'd encourage you to scout around the whole area and find a composition that works for you. Although don't be bashful about replicating the iconic shots you've seen many times… Bamburgh Castle and Dunstanburgh Castle spring to mind… there's a reason they're iconic!

Berwick-upon-Tweed **1** **2** **3**

31

B6354 B6525 B6353

Lowick **32**

A1

Holy Island of Lindisfarne **4-8**

9 **10** Bamburgh

B1340

Seahouses

Wooler **11** Beadnell

A697

12
Embleton **13**
14 Dunstanburgh
Craster

B6346 B1340 B1339 **15-18**
19

NORTHUMBERLAND
NATIONAL PARK

Alnwick **34**

B6341 **20** Alnmouth

36 A1

35 **21** Amble

37 Rothbury **22**

B6341 A697 Druridge Bay

38 A1068

NORTHUMBERLAND **23** Cresswell

Ashington **24** Newbiggin-by-the-Sea

Morpeth **25**

A696 A189 **26** Blyth

A1 **27** Seaton Sluice

A68 **28** Whitley Bay

A19 **29**
30 Tynemouth

A679 Chollerford Newcastle upon Tyne

Corbridge A69

R. Tyne

Hexham

Please see the next page for locations 39–50.

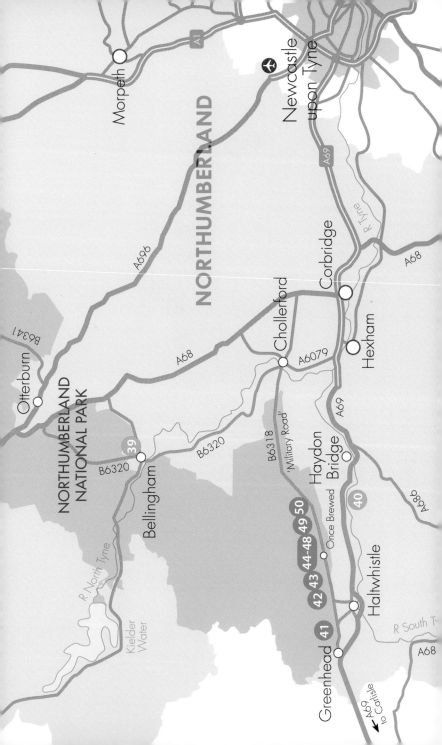

1

The Coast Part 1 – Berwick to Holy Island

Berwick-Upon-Tweed is the northernmost town in England, being just a couple of miles from the Scottish border. It has a traditional market town feel and a lovely situation at the mouth of the River Tweed, with various bridges criss-crossing the water. And just to the south of Berwick you'll find a couple of photographically-interesting beaches – Cocklawburn Beach in particular has some fabulous geology for seascapes.

However, the jewel on this stretch of coast, and a must-visit location in my opinion, is the Holy Island of Lindisfarne (often called just Holy Island). The island is accessed by a tidal causeway and although it's less than two square miles it packs a punch when it comes to photography locations. The castle is one of the most iconic in Northumberland, and along with the ruined priory, harbour and causeway there's plenty to entertain any photographer. If you want to branch out from the classic locations and stretch your legs, the island is easy walking and sports dunes, mudflats, salt marshes and a mixed shoreline of rocky outcrops and sandy beaches. I'd suggest wandering to Emmanuel Head on the northeastern tip, but the area around Snook Point on the western cusp is interesting too. For those of you also into wildlife photography, much of the island is a nature reserve and rich in birdlife.

The causeway that links the island to the mainland is impassable twice a day for five or six hours around high tide. Safe crossing times for traffic are posted at either end of the causeway and can also be found online at www.lindisfarne.org.uk. Do be aware that weather conditions can affect the safe crossing times, so don't cut it too close, especially if it's stormy (a car is stranded on the causeway roughly once a month and is very expensive to rescue!). You can find high and low tide times online for planning photography shoots – see page 115. These come from various tide stations on the coast and handily there's one on Holy Island.

Unsurprisingly the island is a popular tourist destination, so if you're looking for tranquillity aim to visit in low-season or stay overnight on the island when there are far fewer visitors. Having said that, sunrise and sunset are generally quiet at any time of year.

4

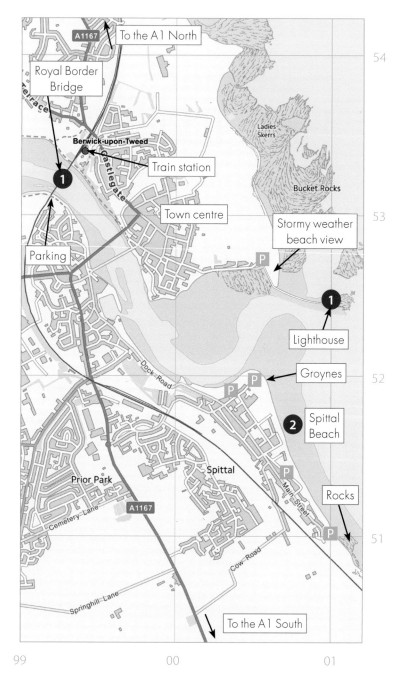

To the A1 North

A1167

Royal Border
Bridge

Berwick-upon-Tweed

Train station

Town centre

Stormy weather
beach view

Parking

Lighthouse

Groynes

Spittal
Beach

Prior Park

Spittal

Rocks

A1167

Cemetery Lane

Cow Road

Springhill Lane

Ladies
Skerrs

Bucket Rocks

Dock Road

Main Street

To the A1 South

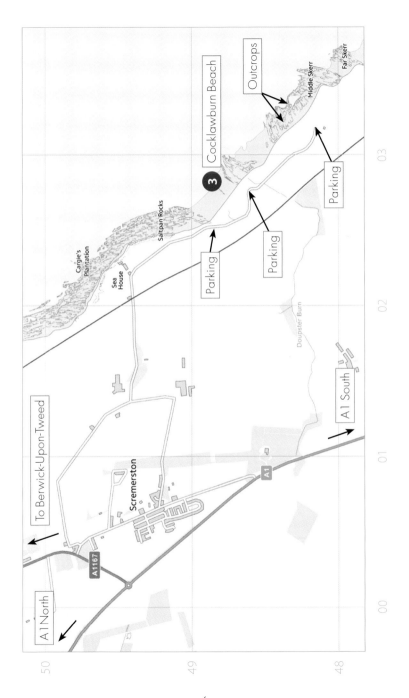

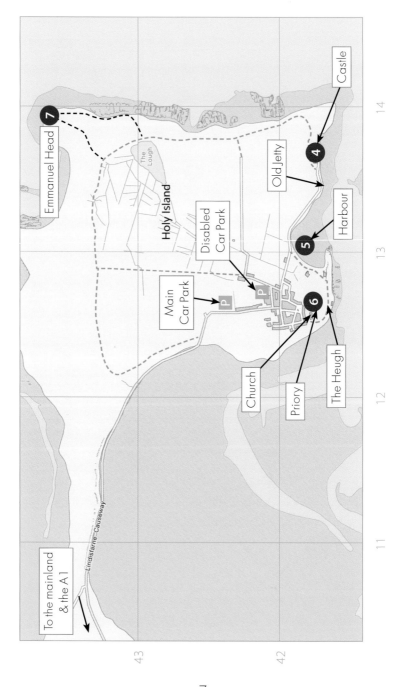

Castle

Old Jetty

Harbour

4

5

Holy Island

The Lough

Disabled Car Park

Main Car Park

Emmanuel Head

7

Church

Priory

The Heugh

6

To the mainland & the A1

Lindisfarne Causeway

14

13

12

11

43

42

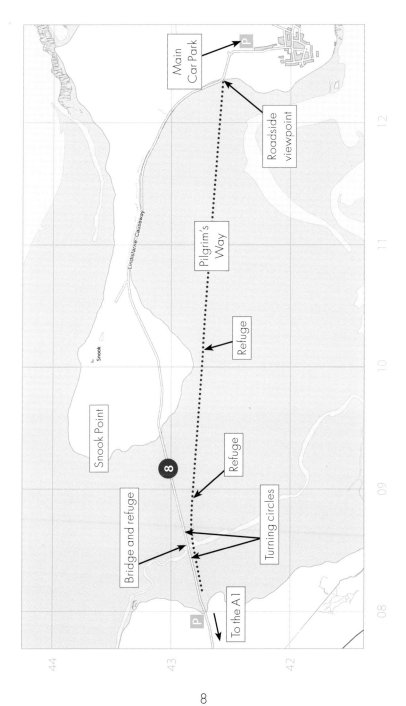

1 BERWICK-UPON-TWEED

There are two locations of photographic interest in Berwick that I'd recommend – the Royal Border Bridge (shown below) and Berwick Lighthouse (pictured on the right).

The Royal Border Bridge is a 660-metre long railway viaduct that spans the River Tweed. It was built in the mid-1800s and the high curved arches look fantastic reflected in the river, especially at night when it's floodlit. Aim to visit around high tide when the estuary is full and so more of the viaduct is captured in the water (there's a tide station at Berwick, so use those tide times). You can shoot it from both the east and west river bank, and both areas are equally good.

Berwick Lighthouse sits at the end of a long stone pier and is striking in its simplicity. The textured surface of the pier makes interesting foreground and there are also a few metal mooring posts dotted around for added interest. My favourite composition is from on top of the wide pier wall, using it as a leading line, but it is a bit of a jump to get up onto. (Avoid low tide for this as it works better with water on both sides of the pier.) You need a strong sky at this location for a good photo and it's generally best at sunrise. The pier and lighthouse also look very dramatic in heavy seas with the waves crashing into them – you can capture the scene in safety from the small beach to the north.

» How to get there

For the bridge on the western side, from the A1167 follow the signs for "Tweed Dock" and when you reach the river turn left and follow the road that goes under the bridge. Take the next right onto Riverside Road and you can park at the end of the road or directly under the arches of the viaduct. For the eastern side, the best place to park is the train station car park (Pay & Display), although there is some free parking on the main road nearby. Go down the steps by the bus stop in the station car park and follow the path down through Castle Vale Park to the riverfront, which takes about five minutes.

For the lighthouse, follow the main road down through the town centre. After the town hall (the one with the clock tower) go straight on instead of following the one-way system round to the right. Turn right at the end of the road, then take the next left onto Ness Street and you'll pass under an archway onto the waterfront. Continue along the waterfront and you'll find a small parking area at the end (free). If that's full there's more free parking down the lane on the left. It's an 8-minute walk along the pier to the lighthouse.

» Grid references

NT 992 531 for the western side of the bridge (nearest postcode TD15 2HQ), NT 994 532 for the eastern side (the train station postcode is TD15 1NF), NU 005 527 for lighthouse parking (postcode TD15 1JB), NU 011 524 for the lighthouse itself.

2 SPITTAL BEACH

Spittal Beach lies just to the south of Berwick, on the other side of the River Tweed, and although the surrounding area isn't the most alluring there are a couple of attractions for photographers. The main draw is a scattering of wooden groynes, which look fantastic with the sea washing over them. Berwick Lighthouse is also visible in the background, adding an extra point of interest to the scene, but it also makes a great subject in itself – placing the harbour wall on the horizon with an interesting sky behind and the sea in front creates a strong minimalist composition. In addition to the views, there's a small outcrop of eroded layered sandstone, which is perfect for abstracts, with beautiful lines and curves in a multitude of muted colours (shown below). If you want to shoot the groynes aim for high tide, for the rocks aim for low tide (the nearest tide station is Berwick).

» How to get there

The groynes are at the northern end of the beach and there's a free car park right next to them. The sandstone rocks are at the other end of the beach, which is a 15-minute walk, or you can park at the end of the main street by the football pitch (also free). See the map on page 5 for details.

» Grid references

NU 005 520 for the car park near the groynes (nearest postcode TD15 1RE), NU 011 510 for the rocks.

3 COCKLAWBURN BEACH

This beach is three miles south of Berwick-Upon-Tweed, near the village of Scremerston, and has some exceptionally photogenic geology. The sandy shore is punctuated by rock shelves jutting out into the sea and there's a wealth of them to explore along the length of the beach. Two of my favourite areas are a limestone block pavement (pictured above) and an outcrop of furrows that look fantastic with the sea flowing down the grooves. The location is best at sunrise and there's plenty to photograph whatever the tide height. If you want to shoot the block pavement around high tide is ideal (the nearest tide station to here is Berwick). If it's the furrows you want to capture aim for half way between high and low tide.

» How to get there

At the roundabout on the A1 just south of Berwick, take the turning to Berwick onto the A1167. Take the next right turn you come to, signed "Scremerston", then almost immediately turn left, signposted "Cocklawburn Beach". Follow the lane along and take a final left, signposted "Beach". There are plenty of parking areas by the shore, although the road to the furthest one is a bit bumpy. See the map on page 6 for the location of the outcrops mentioned.

» Grid references

NU 028 486 for parking (nearest postcode TD15 2RJ).

4 LINDISFARNE CASTLE

Built in the 16th century this iconic castle sits proudly atop a volcanic outcrop at the southeastern end of Holy Island. It's not the most elaborate of castles on the Northumberland coastline, but its remarkable setting and sheer variety of foreground do make it one of the most photogenic. There's a wooden fence along the shoreline that makes a superb leading line to the castle (pictured on the right), and the winding cobbled entrance road can be used to the same effect. On the shore you'll also find some eroded wooden posts – remnants of an old jetty that served the lime kiln industry on the island in the 19th century. These make fantastic foreground, although they are slowly succumbing to the power of the sea and only a few remain. Near the posts you'll also find some rusty mooring rings attached to the rock, which are a favourite foreground element with many photographers (shown on the far right). It's a fabulous location at any time of year and no matter what the tide height there are plenty of compositions to explore, although if you want to shoot the old jetty posts or mooring rings avoid the peak of high tide. (There's a tide station on Holy Island.) As for time of day, sunrise is a terrific time to visit.

» How to get there

Visitors are encouraged to park in the main car park on the island (Pay & Display), which is on the

left before the village. There is a car park closer to the village for disabled badge holders (see the map on page 7 for the location). From the main car park, turn left and follow the road into the village. When the road swings sharply left, go straight on, then turn left at the next junction and this road will take you all the way to the castle. It's a flat 15-minute walk from the car park. The castle is managed by the National Trust and is open to visitors if you want to go inside. See www.national trust.org.uk/lindisfarne-castle for prices and opening hours. During castle opening hours there's a regular shuttle bus that'll take you from the car park to the castle, via the village, for a small fee. You'll find the old jetty posts and mooring rings to the right of the gateway just before the castle.

» Grid references

NU 126 424 for the main car park (nearest postcode TD15 2SE), NU 135 417 for the old posts and mooring rings.

5 HOLY ISLAND HARBOUR

Holy Island has a small natural harbour, known locally as The Ouse. It's still home to a few commercial shellfish vessels, but you'll find small fishing boats and sailing boats moored in the harbour too. When the tide is in the moored boats look fabulous reflected in the sea with the castle providing a spectacular backdrop. If the tide is out you can still explore similar compositions, but be prepared to get muddy feet if you want to get close to the boats.

Scattered along the shore you'll also find the usual jumble of maritime paraphernalia, such as coils of rope, lobster pots and buoys. This gives you plenty of foreground choice for wider shots as well as numerous possibilities for inner landscapes.

One of the most popular subjects in the harbour is the traditional boat sheds. These are made from the upturned hulls of herring boats that are no longer seaworthy and are usually clad in canvas and tar with timber ribs. Two of the boat sheds are particularly enticing, as they're isolated from the others, giving you a clean composition with the castle in the background (pictured on the right). Those of them in slight disrepair are packed with character and so also great for abstract close-up compositions. Shots of the boat sheds work very well in black and white, and an interesting sky

helps significantly with wide-angle shots. (There are three more boat sheds just behind the castle, but these are well maintained so less interesting than those in the harbour.) All the views are looking eastwards, so aim to be there at sunrise if you can. Sunset is also worth a try as the warm evening light illuminates the castle in the background.

» How to get there

Park in the main car park on the island, which is on the left before the village (Pay & Display). There is a car park closer to the village for disabled badge holders (see the map on page 7 for the location). From the main car park, turn left and follow the road into the village. When the road swings sharply left, go straight on, then turn left at the next junction and this road will take you to the harbour. It takes about 8 minutes from the car park. The two most popular boat sheds are the ones closest to the road that leads to the castle.

» Grid references

NU 126 424 for the main car park (nearest postcode TD15 2SE), NU 130 419 for the harbour.

6 LINDISFARNE PRIORY

This small monastery was founded in the 6th century and has a long and complex history, although only ruins now remain. It's open to the public if you want to explore the architecture inside (an entrance fee is payable). There's also a delightful view of the priory from the graveyard of St Mary's Church next door, with the castle just visible in the background. Furthermore, St Mary's has some interesting features to do detail shots of, such as stained-glass windows, multi-coloured sandstone brickwork and celtic crosses. For a higher vantage point, an excellent location is the hill to the south of the ruins, known as The Heugh. This area is particularly attractive in the summer when the wildflowers are blooming. Finally, I'd recommend exploring the views of the priory from the harbour, using assorted fishing equipment as foreground (shown above).

» How to get there

From the main car park, follow the road into the village. When the road swings sharply left, go straight on and follow the signs to the priory. See www.english-heritage.org.uk for opening times and ticket prices. The entrance to the churchyard is beside the priory and for The Heugh take the path behind the church or the path from the harbour.

» Grid references

NU 126 424 for the main car park (nearest postcode TD15 2SE), NU 126 418 for the priory.

7 EMMANUEL HEAD

On Emmanuel Head at the north-eastern tip of Holy Island is a striking white pyramidal beacon. It was built in 1810 to aid maritime navigation and stands at a massive 10 metres high. Sitting right beside the shore and edged by rolling grassy dunes it makes an unusual subject. Sadly there's nothing in the background though, so an interesting sky or good light is essential here. It's suitable for sunrise or sunset and is most attractive in summer (as well as being a great place to escape the crowds), but is still good at other times of year, especially with moody skies and shot black and white.

» How to get there

From the main island car park, walk into the village and make your way to the castle. Take the path around the left-hand side of the castle and when you get to a footbridge over the path go up onto the embankment. Turn left and continue along the path, keeping beside the fence. When you reach the hide by the little lake, bear right onto the small path across the field. Turn left when you reach the shore and continue along to the point. It's a pleasant flat walk and takes about 30 minutes from the castle (45 from the main car park).

» Grid references

NU 126 424 for the main car park (nearest postcode TD15 2SE), NU 139 436 for the beacon.

8 HOLY ISLAND CAUSEWAY

The causeway that links the mainland to Holy Island is often overlooked in the excitement to get to the island, but it's an interesting area that's well worth exploring. Running alongside the causeway on the southern side is a line of tall wooden posts that mark the route of the Pilgrims' Way – an ancient walking trail for pilgrims crossing the sands to the monastery. These posts make a marvellous minimalist subject and look superb when the tide is out and they're reflected in the wet sand, as well as semi-submerged when the tide is in (pictured below). There are also two timber refuge huts for walkers caught out by the tide along this route, which are fascinating subjects in their own right (pictured on the right). There are interesting photographic opportunities on the main causeway too, particularly the bridge section, which has a tall white refuge hut next to it for car drivers. This looks great from the side with the refuge providing an unusual focal point, as well as from on the road using the railings as leading lines. Whatever you're shooting at this location, sunrise is generally best from the mainland side and sunset from the island.

» How to get there

On the mainland, just before the causeway starts, there's a small free car park on the left. There are

also a few small turning circles along the first stretch of causeway where you can park temporarily.

The posts are most easily photographed from either end of the causeway. For the mainland side, park in the car park or a turning circle and walk along the causeway until you find a view you like. If you want to shoot directly along the line of posts you'll have to walk out onto the sands, which can be very muddy. On the island side, the posts reach all the way to the shore, so you can shoot from the roadside without getting your feet dirty. This location is just a short walk down the road from the main island car park.

If you do venture out onto the sands be aware that the tide comes in very fast here and the current can be strong enough to push a car off the road, so always aim to be off the sands at least 2 hours before the causeway closes to traffic.

Only one of the two refuge huts on the Pilgrims' Way is easily accessible, being just 250 metres from the road. Park in the turning circle after the bridge and walk across the sands to it. Again, be prepared to get muddy feet. (The other refuge is much further from any parking areas and only recommended if you can make the round trip on a falling tide.)

» Grid references

NU 079 427 for the car park on the mainland, NU 126 424 for the island car park (nearest postcode TD15 2SE). See the map on page 8 for the locations of the bridge and refuges.

2

The Coast Part 2 – Bamburgh to Alnmouth

This entire stretch of coastline is part of the Northumberland Coast Area of Outstanding Natural Beauty (AONB), and it's well-deserving of the accolade. There are miles of sublime sandy beaches, and combined with the swathes of grass-covered dunes and rugged rocky headlands, it's a seascape photographer's paradise. It's also home to two of the most iconic castles in Northumberland – Bamburgh and Dunstanburgh. They're classic locations with an irresistible mix of striking heritage and stunning surroundings. Unsurprisingly, both are extremely popular with photographers, so expect to have company, even in the depths of winter.

Much of the dramatic scenery along this section of coast is due to an underlying sheet of hard igneous rock called dolerite (or whinstone). This vast sheet, known as the Whin Sill, is present under much of Northumberland but is exposed along the shore here. Both Bamburgh Castle and Dunstanburgh Castle owe their commanding settings to dolerite outcrops, but venture just south of Craster and you'll find even more scenery shaped by this geology that's just as impressive, with many great locations for powerful seascapes.

The Northumberland Coast Path runs all the way down the coastline, making it a very accessible area with easy walking. It's all a delight to wander along, but I'd highly recommend the stretch between Embleton Bay and Howick. Dotted along the shoreline are plenty of pretty villages and sleepy hamlets too – Bamburgh, Beadnell, Low Newton-by-the-Sea, Craster and Alnmouth are all quite charming (with Beadnell and Craster having small traditional harbours). The area can get very busy in the summer, but if you want a bit of solitude there are quieter places, such as Budle Bay or Sugar Sands.

Finally, the Farne Islands lie just off the coast between Bamburgh and Seahouses and are one of the best places in the UK to photograph puffins, seabirds and seals. Boat trips run from Seahouses throughout the year – May to the end of July is the best time for puffins, and seals can be seen year-round, but aim for October/November to see pups.

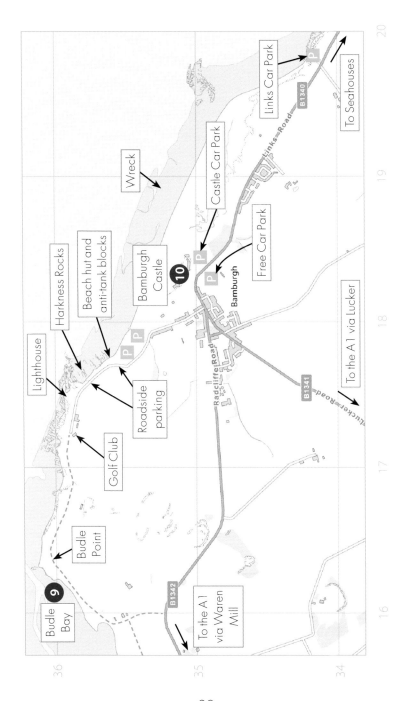

Lighthouse

Harkness Rocks

Beach hut and anti-tank blocks

Wreck

Bamburgh Castle

Castle Car Park

Links Car Park

To Seahouses

Links Road

B1340

Roadside parking

Golf Club

Budle Point

9 Budle Bay

B1342

To the A1 via Waren Mill

Radcliffe Road

Bamburgh

Free Car Park

10

Lucker Road

B1341

To the A1 via Lucker

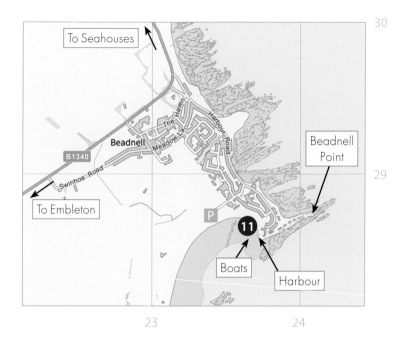

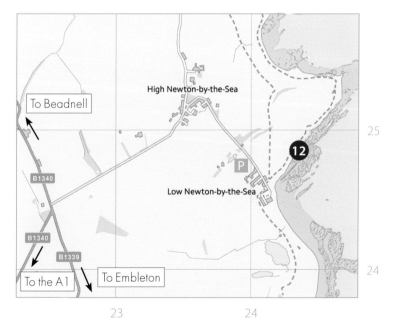

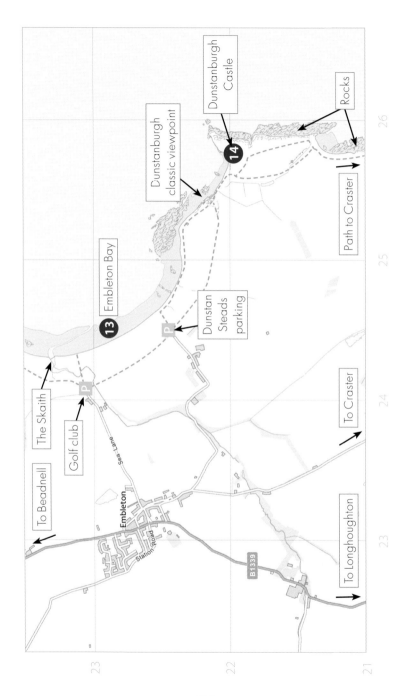

To Beadnell

The Skaith

Golf club

Sea Lane

Embleton

Station Road

To Longhoughton

B1339

To Craster

Dunstan Steads parking

13 Embleton Bay

Dunstanburgh classic viewpoint

Dunstanburgh Castle

14

Rocks

Path to Craster

26

25

24

23

22

21

23

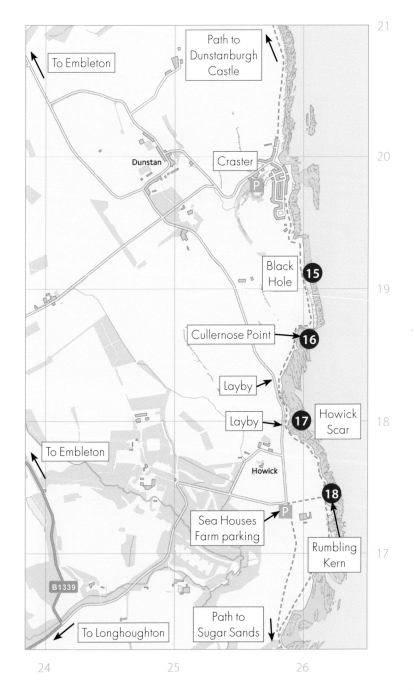

To Embleton

Path to
Dunstanburgh
Castle

Dunstan

Craster

P

Black
Hole **15**

Cullernose Point **16**

Layby

Layby **17** Howick
Scar

To Embleton

Howick

18

Sea Houses
Farm parking P

Rumbling
Kern

B1339

To Longhoughton

Path to
Sugar Sands

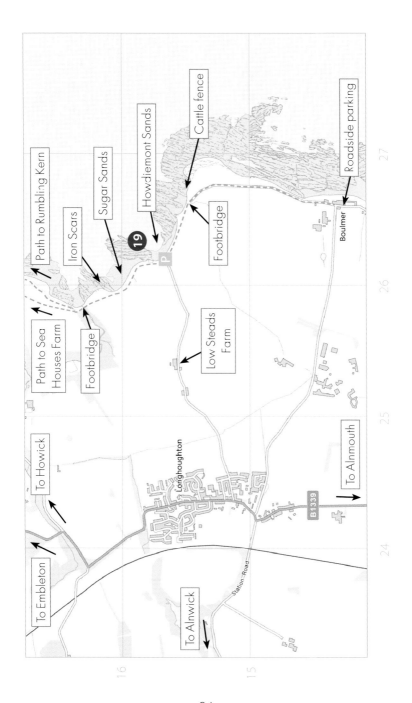

Path to Rumbling Kern

Iron Scars

Sugar Sands

Howdiemont Sands

Cattle fence

Roadside parking

19

Footbridge

Boulmer

Path to Sea Houses Farm

Footbridge

Low Steads Farm

To Howick

To Alnmouth

Longhoughton

To Embleton

B1339

To Alnwick

Station Road

27

26

25

24

16

15

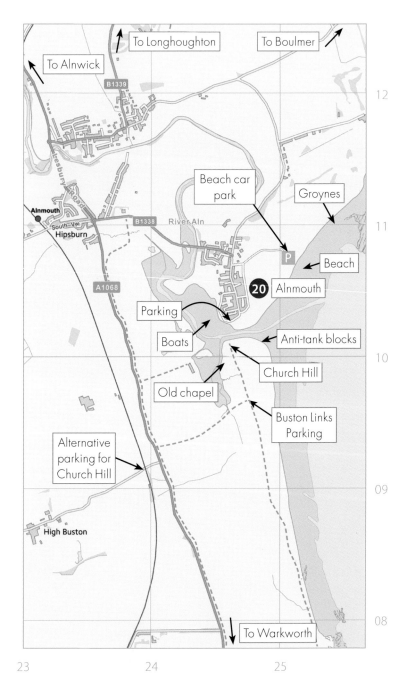

9 BUDLE BAY

This vast bay lies to the north of Bamburgh and the view from Budle Point across the estuary to Ross Back Sands is wonderful, although the many opportunities for inner landscapes are a huge draw here too. The shore is edged by high dunes, giving you endless possible compositions of sand, sky and marram grass to explore. At low tide even more is on offer as drainage channels appear in the estuary, winding their way to the sea, and the retreating waves reveal sand ripples and pools. This tranquil area is a great place to escape the crowds in summer and is best at sunset. (N.B. no matter how tempting, it's not safe to cross the mouth of the estuary.)

» How to get there

From Bamburgh, take the small lane behind the castle. It's on the left if you're coming from the A1 (signed "The Wynding") and on the right if coming from Seahouses (signed "Golf course"). There are two free car parks in the dunes along here and roadside parking towards the end of the lane. Continue along the road on foot to the golf club and when you reach it take the path on the right that skirts the shoreline, or if the tide is out just walk along the beach. It takes about 25 minutes to get to Budle Point.

» Grid references

NU 176 357 for parking (postcode NE69 7DE), NU 163 361 for Budle Point.

10 BAMBURGH CASTLE

As quintessential as they come, Bamburgh Castle is a magnet for photographers, and with very good reason – it's a magnificent building in a spectacular setting and easily accessible. Fronted by acres of golden sand and flanked by grassy dunes there are plenty of different viewpoints to explore.

One of the most popular areas to shoot the castle from is Harkness Rocks, just to the northwest. You'll find a huge variety of ledges, rocky outcrops and tidal pools here, giving you an endless choice of foreground to compliment the view (pictured above). There's plenty to work with

whatever the height of the tide, such as reflections in rock pools at low tide or waves surging over the ledges near high tide. Just beside the rocks is Bamburgh Lighthouse, which is a great subject in itself. The tiny white building has a walled enclosure and there's an attractive composition from the top of the hill looking down the winding line of steps to it. And if you wander along the beach from the rocks towards the castle you'll also find a tiny beach hut and some World War II anti-tank blocks that provide yet more foreground interest.

There are also many attractive viewpoints from within the sand dunes. The long marram grass is a delightful element to include, especially with a bit of wind creating some movement in long exposures. There are dunes on both sides of the castle, but my favourite area is on the northwest side, which is a great location at sunset as the golden light illuminates the castle (pictured below). Having said that, in the summer months you'll also find plenty of wildflowers, such as poppies and lupins, in the links area behind the dunes to the southeast of the castle. These add interest and a splash of colour to any scene and are usually at their peak in June.

When the tide is retreating and the sand is wet you can get some fabulous reflections of the castle in the beach (shown on the next page). There's no particular area that's best for this, it's just a case of finding a patch that's reflective.

It's a very popular beach though, so it can be tricky to get something without people in. You can either embrace the people and add them to your composition or go very early!

There's also an old boat wreck on the beach to the south of the castle that periodically appears and disappears with the shifting sands. If you're lucky and it's visible when you visit, the ribs of the hull make great foreground.

Bamburgh is undoubtedly a superb location for sunrise, but it's also well worth visiting for sunset. You can either shoot into the sunset from the beach on the southeast side, or shoot the warm sidelight on the landscape from the northwest. The nearest tide station is North Sunderland, so use those tide times to plan your visit.

» How to get there

For Harkness Rocks, take the small lane behind the castle. If you're coming from Seahouses it's on the right after you pass the castle and village green (signed "Golf course"). If you're coming from the A1 it's on the left before you reach the castle (signed "The Wynding"). There are two small car parks in the dunes along here (both free) and roadside parking right in front of the rocks. For the southern end of the beach there are many car parks nearby – one at the castle (at the time of writing, £2 all day), one opposite the castle (free) and one further towards Seahouses (£2 all day). See the map on page 22 for the exact locations. It's just a short walk through the dunes to the beach from any of them.

» Grid references

NU 177 357 for Harkness Rocks (nearest postcode NE69 7DE), NU 189 352 for the wreck. The castle postcode is NE69 7DF.

11 BEADNELL

With the only west-facing harbour on the east coast, the small village of Beadnell is a great location for sunset. The harbour sits at the northern tip of a pretty crescent-shaped sandy bay and is backed by characterful old lime kilns. As well as shooting out across the harbour into the setting Sun (pictured on the right) you can also capture it bathed in warm light from the end of the harbour wall, or take in the wider scene from the beach. If you're shooting across the harbour, it looks much

more attractive when full, with the boats and sky reflected in the water, so aim to visit around high tide if you can. Another subject for high tide is the stone jetty that juts out from the end of the harbour wall. This makes an excellent minimalist seascape with the water lapping over it. You'll find the usual fishing gear strewn around the area, which is great for detail shots, and for much of the year there are also sailing boats moored on the beach, which can be interesting to explore when the tide is out. Finally, Beadnell Point is also worthy of attention for traditional seascapes, with a long limestone slab tapering out into the sea. It's better at sunrise than sunset and is suitable at any tide height. The nearest tide station to Beadnell is North Sunderland.

» How to get there

Beadnell is just off the B1340, 2½ miles south of Seahouses. Turn off the B1340 and continue through the village. Ignore the left turn to the harbour and you'll find a free car park on the left by the beach. It's a 2-minute walk along the shore to the harbour. Beadnell Point is behind the lime kilns – take the path that runs between the lime kilns and the buildings, and follow it along for another 3 or 4 minutes.

» Grid references

NU 235 288 for the car park (nearest postcode NE67 5EE), NU 237 286 for the harbour, NU 240 287 for Beadnell Point.

12 LOW NEWTON-BY-THE-SEA

Just a short stroll along the coast from the sleepy hamlet of Low Newton-by-the-Sea is a fantastic stretch of limestone pavement that slopes gently into the sea. It's been weathered over millennia to create a jigsaw-like pattern of rocks, with grooves and potholes, giving you endless choice of foreground. It's particularly photogenic with the sea swirling through the cracks. Sunrise is an ideal time to visit and about one hour either side of high tide (the nearest tide station is North Sunderland). Access is straightforward, being down a gentle banking from the coast path.

» How to get there

From the B1340/B1339 coastal road between Beadnell and Embleton, take the turning to "Newton by the sea". Bear right at High Newton and continue to Low Newton. There's no parking in the village itself, so park in the small car park on the brow of the hill just before it (Pay & Display). Walk down the hill towards the sea and just before the bottom go through the kissing gate on the left, signed "Newton Point". Follow the lower path and you'll find the start of the pavement after the first stile. It takes about 12 minutes from the car park.

» Grid references

NU 240 248 for the car park (nearest postcode NE66 3EL), NU 244 249 for the pavement.

13 EMBLETON BAY

When the tide is out at Embleton Bay an expanse of golden sand is revealed, giving you a variety of compositions to explore with Dunstanburgh Castle providing a pleasing backdrop in the distance at the southern end of the bay. Compositions that work well include waves rolling across the beach, reflections in the wet shore or sand ripples, which can be used to great effect as leading lines. One of the most interesting areas to investigate is the Skaith, where Embleton Burn flows into the sea (see the map on page 24 for the location). The river can be used to add interest to the scene or you can capture the reflections of the castle in the flat water. Sunrise is an ideal time to visit, but avoid high tide.

» How to get there

The bay is to the east of Embleton village and there are two places to park near the beach – Dunstan Steads and Embleton Golf Club. For Dunstan Steads, turn off the B1339 at Embleton towards Craster. After quarter of a mile turn left to Dunstan Steads and at the end of the lane you'll find roadside parking and a path to the sea. For the golf club, turn into Embleton where you see a brown golf course sign and go straight on at the top of the hill. At the end of the lane you'll find the golf club and a path to the beach. There's limited roadside parking, but you can also park in the club car park for a small fee.

» Grid references

NU 245 224 for Dunstan Steads parking (postcode NE66 3DT), NU 240 230 for the golf club (postcode NE66 3XQ).

14 DUNSTANBURGH CASTLE

Standing proud on the headland between Embleton Bay and the village of Craster are the iconic ruins of Dunstanburgh Castle. Built in the 1300s the only structures to remain largely intact are Lilburn Tower and the grand gatehouse.

The classic view is from the southern end of Embleton Bay, where you'll find a collection of large dark rounded dolerite boulders. These make stunning foreground to compliment Lilburn Tower on the clifftop in the background (pictured below). The boulders look superb with the sea washing over them at mid to high tide, as well as when the tide is out.

The boulders do look better when wet though, so visiting on a falling tide is preferable. N.B. they can be very slippery! (The nearest tide station to here is North Sunderland.) Sunrise is an ideal time to visit, but it's also well worth going for sunset.

The castle itself is under the care of English Heritage and there's an entrance fee to go inside. Visit www.english-heritage.org.uk for info on opening times and prices. You can shoot the grand entrance gates up-close from the footpath, but you need a strong sky or good light for a decent shot here.

The view from the southern side of the castle is often unfairly overlooked. I'll admit it's not quite as spectacular as from the north, but it's attractive nonetheless and much quieter at peak photography

times. Long views across the farmland work well and there are various rocky outcrops along this coastline that make pleasing foreground (pictured above). I've pointed out two of my favourite rocky areas on the map on p.24, but it's a case of wandering along until you find something you like.

» How to get there

The castle can be reached from either Embleton Bay to the north or from Craster to the south. For Embleton Bay, turn off the B1339 at Embleton towards Craster. After quarter of a mile turn left to Dunstan Steads and at the end of the lane you'll find roadside parking. Go through the gate and straight on towards the beach, then take the path on the right that goes along the edge of the golf course. It takes about 15 minutes to get to the classic viewpoint and another 8 minutes to the castle gates.

For Craster, park in the village car park, which is on the right as you enter the village (Pay & Display). Walk down the road to the harbour and turn left. Follow the road along and go through the gate at the end onto the shoreline path. It's just over 1 ¼ miles to the castle gates and takes about 35 minutes.

» Grid references

NU 245 224 for Dunstan Steads parking (postcode NE66 3DT), NU 255 221 for the classic view, NU 256 198 for Craster car park (postcode NE66 3TW).

15 BLACK HOLE

Just to the south of the village of Craster is a rocky inlet known as Black Hole. A large isolated chunk of rock juts out vertically from the sea bed here, and while it's fairly unassuming to look at, it makes a wonderful seascape with the waves crashing around it at high tide. (The nearest tide station to here is Amble.) Sunrise is the prime time to visit, but it looks very atmospheric under menacing skies and is also suitable at sunset if there's some colour in the clouds.

» How to get there

There are two ways to reach Black Hole – along the coastal path from Craster or along the coastal path from the south. From Craster, park in the car park (on the right as you enter the village – Pay & Display) and walk down the road to the harbour. Turn right at the harbour then left before the Jolly Fisherman pub. Go through the beer garden onto the coastal path and follow it along the coast. Alternatively, you can park in the layby near Cullernose Point to the south (see the map on page 25 for the location). Cross the road and turn left onto the coastal path. It takes 15-20 minutes from either direction.

» Grid references

NU 256 198 for Craster car park (postcode NE66 3TW), NU 258 183 for the Cullernose layby (nearest postcode NE66 3SU), NU 260 191 for Black Hole.

16 CULLERNOSE POINT

The cliffs of Cullernose Point slope sharply into the sea between the villages of Craster and Howick. The bay at the foot of the cliffs (called Swine Den) is carpeted with large dolerite boulders, similar to those near Dunstanburgh Castle. These make fantastic foreground to the cliffs and also for general seascapes. In the bay you'll find some rather interesting exposed folds of limestone bedrock too (called whale-back folds) and there's plenty of opportunity for detail shots, with rock pools, seaweed and rounded pebbles of various sizes in abundance. The cliff runs almost exactly west to east, so it's best at sunrise in the winter months, when the warm rising sun lights the cliff face. Sunset is worth a try too, but the cliffs won't be lit. As for tide height, aim for mid tide for seascapes and low tide for abstracts.

» How to get there

On the minor road between Craster and Howick you'll find a layby alongside a wall that fits 6 or so cars. Park here, cross the road and turn left onto the coastal path. Follow it along for 5 minutes and where the path dips veer right off the path down onto the shore.

» Grid references

NU 258 183 for the layby (nearest postcode NE66 3SU), NU 260 186 for Swine Den.

17 HOWICK SCAR

This scar near the village of Howick is an ancient geological fault line created millions of years ago by colliding landmasses. Huge forks of layered rock snake out into the sea here, creating some excellent opportunities for long-exposure seascapes. The ideal time to visit is at sunrise and it's most dramatic roughly one hour after high tide when the waves surge between the rocks (the nearest tide station to here is Amble). This is not a place where you want to get caught out by the incoming tide though, as you can be easily cut off while stood on one of the rock ledges and the shoreline is backed by high cliffs, so to be safe I'd only recommend shooting here on a falling tide.

» How to get there

On the minor road between Craster and Howick you'll find a small layby right beside the sea (it's on the left if you're coming from Craster, on the right from Howick) – see the map on page 25 for the exact location. Park here and on the other side of the coastal footpath you'll find a tiny path down the cliffs onto the shore. Although it's short, it is very steep and can be slippery underfoot.

» Grid references

NU 259 181 for the layby and the scar (nearest postcode for satnav NE66 3SU).

18 RUMBLING KERN

The rocky shore around Rumbling Kern has a variety of subjects to offer. Perched on the edge of the rocks is the Bathing House, built in Victorian times for Earl Grey of Howick Hall. It provides a perfect focal point for seascapes and the most appealing foreground is on the northern side where there's a large expanse of interesting rocks sloping into the sea (see above). It's an ideal location for sunrise and suitable at any tide height due to the endless choice of rocks. Rumbling Kern is also one of the best places on the Northumberland coast for rock abstracts. There are swathes of sculpted sandstone and shales, with an amazing array of patterns. It's a photographic treasure trove of curves, lines and colours. Make sure to avoid high tide if this is the aim of your visit (the nearest tide station is Amble).

» How to get there

Park at the parking area by Sea Houses Farm (free), which is on a sharp bend on the minor coastal road between Craster and Howick – see the map on page 25 for the exact location. Follow the footpath down the track to the Bathing House. The best seascape viewpoint is to the left of the house and the most attractive rocks for abstracts are behind it and to the right.

» Grid references

NU 259 173 for parking (postcode NE66 3LH), NU 262 175 for the Bathing House.

19 SUGAR SANDS

There are a myriad of different seascape scenes to be found along the shore at Sugar Sands and neighbouring Howdiemont Sands, with stretches of pristine golden beach and eye-catching rock outcrops in plentiful supply. There's no classic shot here – it's just a case of wandering along until you find a viewpoint you like, although I'm often drawn to Iron Scars, which is on the north side of Sugar Sands and has angled ledges pointing straight out to sea. Another firm favourite is a wire cattle fence that snakes out into the water and is often draped in seaweed (pictured above). Sunrise is the perfect time to

visit and there's plenty to shoot whatever the tide height, but aim for high tide for the fence and mid tide for Iron Scars (the nearest tide station to here is Amble).

» How to get there

The beach is to the east of Longhoughton village and during the day you can park right by the shore near Low Steads Farm. Once in Longhoughton, take the turning opposite the church, signposted "Low Steads Farm", onto Crowlea Road. After ¾ of a mile on this single-track lane you'll come to the farm gates where you pay for parking via an honesty box in the wall (50p at the time of writing). Drive through the farm, continue down the lane and park on the shore. For the fence, walk south (i.e. to the right) along the beach or shoreline path for about 7 minutes and you'll find it just after the small footbridge and walled enclosure. Sugar Sands is to the north (i.e. to the left) and you can either walk along the beach or along the coastal path (you'll find a small trail just past the midpoint of the bay to get down to the beach).

The gate at the end of the lane onto the shore is locked at night though. The time it's locked at varies throughout the year, from 7pm in mid-summer to 4pm mid-winter (the daily time is displayed on the gate at the farm), and it's usually unlocked around 8.30am. There are a few alternatives if you want to visit outside of these times. You can park on the verge at the bottom of the lane at any time and walk through the small gate onto the shore. It is mighty tight to turn a car around on the lane though, so if this is your plan I'd recommend doing a reccy during the day to check you're happy with this. If you arrive before the gates are locked and want to

stay past the closing time you can easily turn around on the shore then park on the lane so you're not locked in. The other alternative is to walk from Boulmer, Howick or Longhoughton. It takes roughly 20 minutes to walk from any of the villages, although the fence is closer to Boulmer and Iron Scars is closer to Howick. If you're walking from Boulmer, park on the roadside by the church, or in the car park a little further along, and walk down the lane on the sharp bend and along the coastal path. If you're walking from Howick, park in the parking area at Sea Houses Farm (see location 18 for a description). Take the track at the far end of the parking area, signed "Public Byway", and follow it down to the sea. Cross the stream using the footbridge and Sugar Sands is over the next hill.

» Grid references

NU 262 156 for Low Steads Farm parking (nearest postcode NE66 3AL), NU 260 162 for Iron Scars, NU 267 155 for the cattle fence.

20 ALNMOUTH

This lovely village lies at the mouth of the River Aln and the winding estuary is dotted with moored fishing boats and sailing boats. These are a great subject to explore, whether the tide is in or out, especially if you can include reflections in your composition.

As you're looking roughly west across the estuary it's a good area for sunset.

On the seaward side of the village there's also a large sandy beach, and at the northern end you'll find a few wooden groynes that look fantastic with the waves washing over them (pictured on the next page). They're best at high tide at sunrise (the nearest tide station to here is Amble).

The finest view at Alnmouth is from the southern side of the river on Church Hill. From this high vantage point you're treated to a wide vista across the estuary to the houses crowded along the waterfront and there's also a large wooden cross, dedicated to St Cuthbert, for interest (pictured on the right). The scene works very well in panoramic format and it's a good location for sunrise, but also a cracking spot for sunset. Around the hill you'll also find a few other subjects of interest – on the shore opposite the village are a few anti-tank blocks from World War II, and on the southwestern side is a roofless old mortuary chapel.

» How to get there

For the estuary, follow the main road through the village and at the bottom of the hill you'll emerge onto the waterfront. Bear right and you'll find plenty of roadside parking, although it can be tricky to find a space in summer.

For the groynes it's best to park at the beach. Take the first left turn as you enter the village onto "The Wynd" and then the first left again to the Beach Car Park. In spring and summer there's a small charge to park here (at the time of writing £1.50 all day). The groynes are a four minute walk north (i.e. left) along the beach or shore path.

You can't get to Church Hill from the village unfortunately (don't try to wade across the estuary!) – you

need to approach from the south. Leave the village and take the A1068 towards Warkworth. Just under a mile after the roundabout you'll find a track on the left, signposted "Public Bridleway Buston Links". The track isn't paved and gets pretty bumpy towards the end. The last part is also prone to flooding at high tide. If you have a four-wheel drive car then head down the track and park at the bottom. From here various paths wind their way across the dunes and mud flats to Church Hill – start from either the metal gate or the footpath signpost. The paths aren't particularly clear and which is the best way to go depends on whether the tide is in or not, but you'll be able to see the hill all the way and it only takes about 10 minutes. Personally, I wouldn't go down the track in a normal car, so if you don't want to risk it, continue along the A1068 towards Warkworth and take the next right turn you come to. On the other side of the railway bridge you'll find space to park on the left. Walk back to the main road, cross over and turn left onto the footpath. Follow it along and turn right onto the Buston Links track. It's about a mile from this parking spot and takes roughly 30 minutes.

» Grid references

NU 247 103 for estuary parking (nearest postcode NE66 2RX), NU 251 107 for the Beach Car Park (nearest postcode NE66 2RB), NU 254 110 for the groynes, NU 247 095 for Buston Links parking, NU 239 091 for the alternative Church Hill parking, NU 246 101 for Church Hill itself.

3
SECTION

The Coast Part 3 – Amble to Tynemouth

The coastline between the village of Amble and the mouth of the River Tyne near Newcastle is much more built-up than in the north, but there are still pockets of rugged scenery and tranquillity to be found. The beaches at Cresswell and Low Hauxley are just two good examples. And if you're intrigued by the simple interplay between sea and sand you'll find seven miles of golden beach and grassy dunes to explore at Druridge Bay.

Due to the area's industrial heritage, maritime economy and the need for coastal defences, there's a stronger presence of man-made structures along this stretch of coast, such as piers, pipes, groynes and breakwaters. Rather than detracting from the beauty of the area they enhance it and serve as wonderful subjects for seascapes. Admittedly, in some places the surroundings are far less romantic than on the northern coast, but the added photographic potential of these features more than makes up for this. There's something to be found at nearly every town or village, but the beach at the bustling port town of Blyth has a large concentration of structures with endless compositions to investigate. That's not to say that natural features are absent on this part of the coast – there's a fabulous sea stack at Seaton Sluice that's one of my personal favourite locations.

The magnificent Northumberland coastline comes to an end at Seaton Sluice, but just over the border in Tyne & Wear are a couple of great coastal locations, so I've also included these at the end of the section. The outright highlight is St Mary's Lighthouse, which has a remarkable setting. It's easily accessible, good from dawn until dusk and there are plenty of viewpoints whatever the tide height.

For those of you also interested in wildlife photography, Coquet Island lies less than a mile off the coast near Amble and is an important bird reserve for terns and puffins. Regular boat trips run from Amble and are best in the summer months. And there's also the Druridge Pools nature reserve at Druridge Bay, which is good for waders and wildfowl.

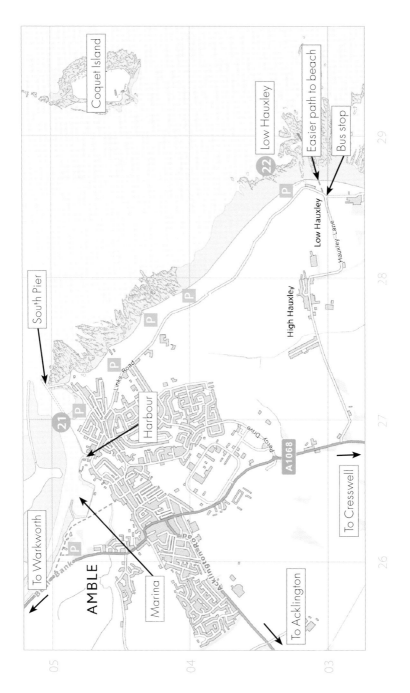

Coquet Island

South Pier

Low Hauxley

Easier path to beach

Bus stop

Low Hauxley

Hauxley Lane

High Hauxley

Links Road

Harbour

Percy Drive

A1068

To Cresswell

To Warkworth

Marina

AMBLE

Acklington Road

To Acklington

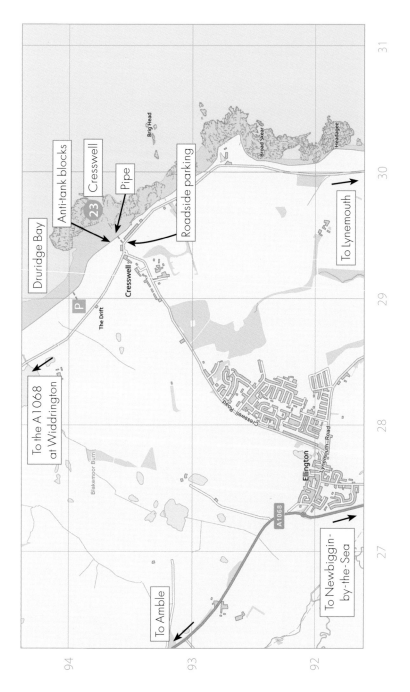

Druridge Bay

Anti-tank blocks

Cresswell

23

Pipe

Roadside parking

Brig Head

Broad Skear

Headagee

To Lynemouth

The Drift

Cresswell

To the A1068
at Widdrington

Blakemoor Burn

Cresswell Road

Ellington

Lynemouth Road

A1068

To Amble

To Newbiggin-
by-the-Sea

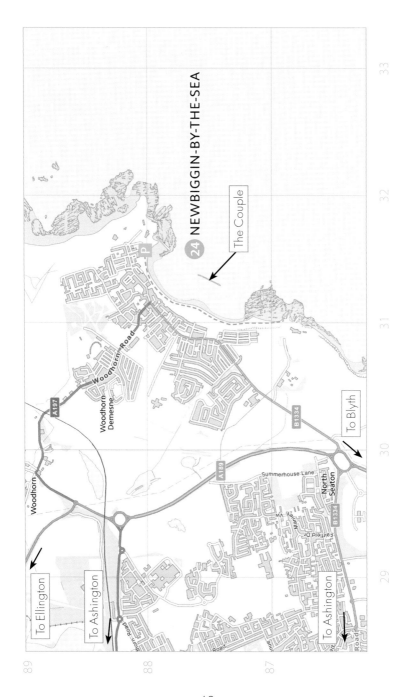

NEWBIGGIN-BY-THE-SEA

24 The Couple

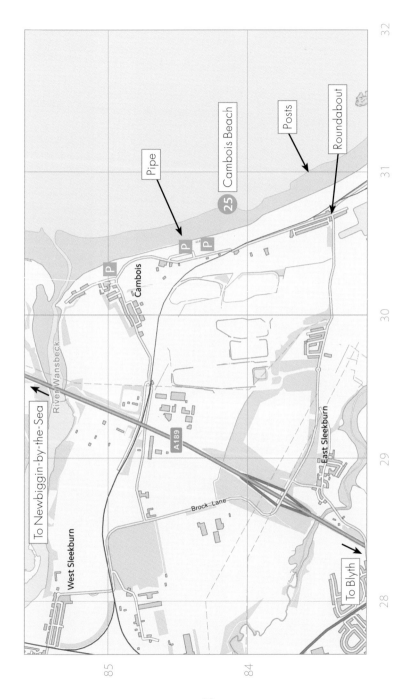

Pipe

Cambois Beach

Posts

Roundabout

25

P

P

P

Cambois

River Wansbeck

To Newbiggin-by-the-Sea

West Sleekburn

A189

Brock Lane

East Sleekburn

To Blyth

32

31

30

29

28

85

84

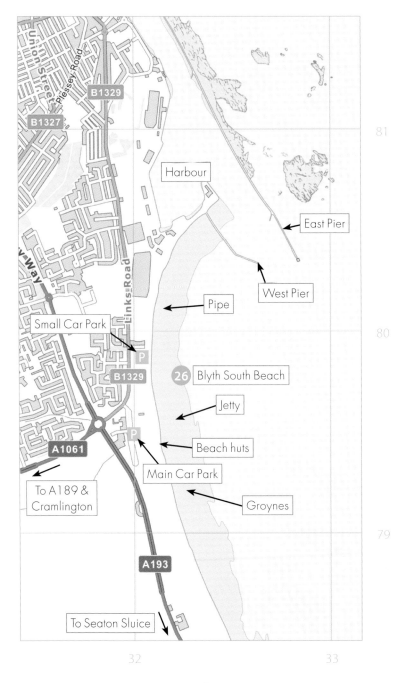

Harbour

East Pier

West Pier

Pipe

Small Car Park

Blyth South Beach 26

Jetty

Beach huts

Main Car Park

Groynes

To A189 & Cramlington

To Seaton Sluice

B1329

B1327

B1329

A1061

A193

Plessey Road

Links Road

Union Street

Way

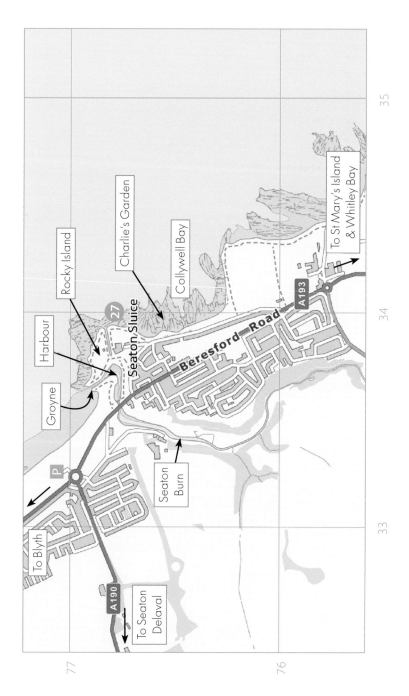

Rocky Island

Charlie's Garden

Collywell Bay

To St Mary's Island
& Whitley Bay

Harbour

Seaton Sluice

Groyne

Beresford Road

A193

Seaton Burn

P

To Blyth

A190

To Seaton Delaval

35

34

33

77

76

51

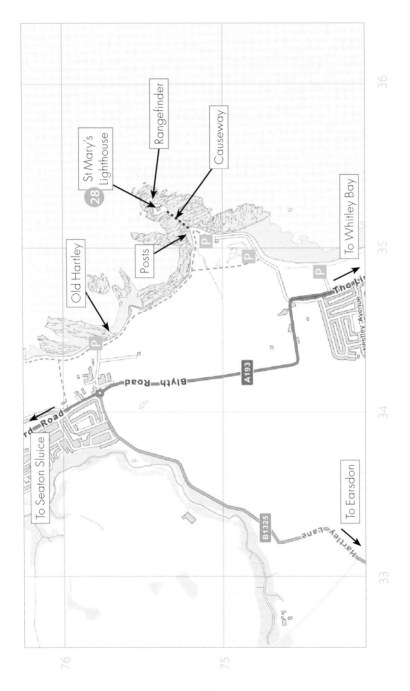

St Mary's Lighthouse

28

Rangefinder

Causeway

Old Hartley

Posts

To Whitley Bay

To Seaton Sluice

Blyth Road

A193

rd Road

To Earsdon

B1325

Hartley Lane

Thornle...

Nestley Avenue

36

35

34

33

76

75

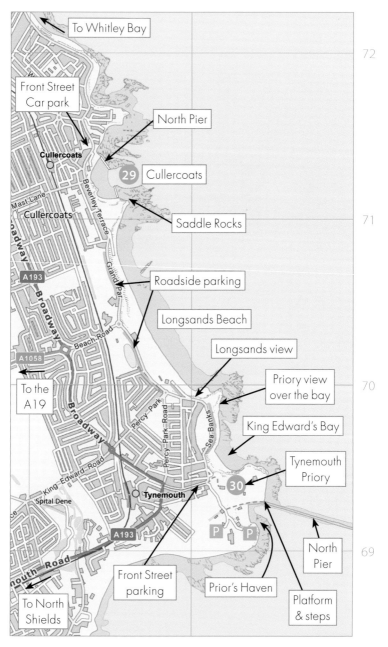

To Whitley Bay

Front Street
Car park

North Pier

Cullercoats

29 Cullercoats

Cullercoats

Saddle Rocks

Mast Lane

Cullercoats

Broadway

A193

Beverley Terrace

Grand Par

Roadside parking

Longsands Beach

Beach Road

A1058

To the
A19

Longsands view

Priory view
over the bay

King Edward's Bay

Tynemouth
Priory

Broadway

Percy Park

Sea Banks

Percy Park Road

King Edward Road

Spital Dene

Tynemouth

30

North
Pier

A193

P   P

outh Road

To North
Shields

Front Street
parking

Prior's Haven

Platform
& steps

21 AMBLE

Although this small town doesn't have the charm that others in the area do, it does have a lovely situation at the mouth of the River Coquet. At the end of the estuary is a marina, small harbour and assortment of piers. It's the South Pier, with its small red and white striped lighthouse, that draws most photographers here. A gate unfortunately prevents access to the very end, but the gaps are wide enough to poke a lens through for a symmetrical shot along the pier with the railings leading the eye in. Another good viewpoint is from the side on the breakwater that connects it to the shore (shown above). There's a small section with a paved stone top that makes a pleasing textured foreground and from some angles you can include nearby Coquet Island on the horizon too. Sunrise and sunset are both good times to visit and it generally looks better when the tide is in (use the times from Amble tide station). If you want to explore further, you'll find moored boats and old jetty remains along the estuary and a wealth of rocky outcrops on the coast to the south.

» How to get there

Amble has a warren of streets, but if you follow the sandcastle symbol on the brown signs from the A1068 you'll get to the waterfront by the pier. There are two Pay & Display car parks here as well as some roadside parking.

» Grid references

NU 272 050 for the South Pier, NU 271 047 for parking (postcode NE65 0AP).

22 LOW HAUXLEY

For classic seascapes you can't go far wrong paying the beach at Low Hauxley a visit. The golden sand is scattered with all manner of interesting rocks, such as lone boulders surrounded by pools of water, fantastic spine-like ridges (pictured below) and even some coated in bright green seaweed if you're lucky. In addition to the wealth of foreground choice, Coquet Island lies less than a mile offshore, adding a point of interest on the horizon. The most alluring rocks are halfway down the beach, so aim for mid tide if you want to capture some wave action (Amble is the nearest tide station). There are still good compositions to be found when the tide is out though. Sunrise is a superb time to visit, but sunset can also be marvellous if there's some colour in the clouds.

» How to get there

From the A1068 just south of Amble, take the turning signposted "Low Hauxley" and follow the road towards the shore. Ignore the right turn by the bus shelter to Low Hauxley – a little further along the road you'll find a small car park in the dunes on your right (free). There's a short but steep descent from the dunes onto the beach. (If you want to avoid the descent, park on the side of the road by the bus shelter and take the small path onto the beach then make your way to the left.)

» Grid references

NU 285 033 for the car park (nearest postcode NE65 0JP).

23 CRESSWELL

Nestled at the southern end of the vast Druridge Bay is the tiny village of Cresswell. On the beach here are various photogenic features, such as a tightly packed line of anti-tank blocks that look fabulous with the waves swirling around them (pictured above), and a narrow concrete-covered pipeline running out to see that makes a striking minimalist composition. Both of these structures are best at high tide (the nearest tide station to here is Amble). There are also plenty of sculpted rock ledges to explore and the grassy dunes lining the bay are beautiful. As usual, sunrise is the best time to visit, although sunset can still be productive, and the blocks and pipe work well with moody skies.

» How to get there

From the A1068 a few miles north of Newbiggin, take the turning at the roundabout to "Ellington", then turn left after ¼ mile to "Cresswell". When you reach Cresswell, turn right at the T-junction and park on the side of the road. The path to the beach is next to Cresswell Ices, opposite the public toilets. If there's nowhere to park on the roadside, drive north along the coast road and you'll find a free car park on the right after 500 metres (N.B. it has a 2-metre height limit). It's an 8-minute walk back down the beach to the blocks, pipe and rocks.

» Grid references

NZ 295 936 for the beach,
NZ 289 939 for the car park
(nearest postcode NE61 5LA).

24 NEWBIGGIN-BY-THE-SEA

Perched on top of a breakwater in the middle of Newbiggin Bay is "The Couple" – a 12-metre high brass sculpture of a man and a woman looking out to sea. My favourite composition is from directly behind it with only the sea and sky as background, but the view from the northern side with the wind turbines of North Blyth in the background also works well (pictured below). The key to a good photo here is a strong sky – whether that's at sunrise, sunset or during a storm. Heavy seas also add drama as the waves crash over the breakwater. The composition is cleanest when the tide is in but it also looks good when the tide is out and the figures are reflected in the wet sand (the nearest tide station is Blyth). It is 300 metres offshore so you'll need a longish lens (100-200mm) to fill the frame.

» How to get there

There's a large free car park at the northern end of the bay, by the church and maritime centre – once in Newbiggin just follow the signs for the "Sea Front" to get to it. From here it's a 10-minute flat walk along the promenade to get directly behind the sculpture. Alternatively, park on the main street and go down one of the side streets onto the promenade.

» Grid references

NZ 317 880 for the car park (postcode NE64 6DB),
NZ 314 876 for The Couple.

25 CAMBOIS BEACH

Although the surrounding area is rather industrial, the long beach at Cambois (pronounced "cammus") is very peaceful and has a couple of photogenic features. The first is a colossal outfall pipe that stretches over 300 metres out into the sea (pictured above). Since it's so long you can shoot it at any tide height, but I prefer high tide (the nearest tide station is Blyth). There are also two sets of tall marker posts on the beach that warn boats of the remains of another old outfall pipe, and these make a striking minimalist subject, as do the wind turbines just offshore. Moody skies compliment the industrial feel very well, but it's also great at sunrise.

» How to get there

From the A189 between Blyth and Newbiggin, take the exit signed "Cambois Beach" and follow the signs to Cambois. At the mini-roundabout near the shore turn left and after half a mile you'll find two small free car parks close together on the right. The pipe is in front of the second car park. The marker posts are a 10-minute walk down the beach towards Blyth (see the map on page 49 for the exact location). Alternatively, park on the side of the road near the mini-roundabout and go through the underpass by it onto the beach right by the posts.

» Grid references

NZ 305 844 for the car parks and pipe (postcode NE24 1RQ), NZ 310 835 for the marker posts.

26 BLYTH

Blyth South Beach is a treasure trove for seascape photography, with a lovely stretch of gently sloping golden sand, a pleasant promenade and various man-made features that could keep any photographer entertained for hours.

In front of the promenade is a short, plain concrete jetty and while this looks pretty unattractive at low tide it's a very graphic subject around high tide with the sea washing over and around it. The most popular composition is looking directly along it out to sea, but from the side also works well.

On the promenade are two rows of multicoloured beach huts. These are a fun subject to shoot,

either close-up or at distance from on the beach, and a blue sky compliments the colours nicely.

Moving north along the beach from the promenade you'll find a large outfall pipe raised on robust wooden struts. Again, you can shoot directly along it or from the side, and mid to high tide is usually a good time. It looks especially attractive when reflected in wet sand.

At the very northern end of the beach are two huge piers, guarding the entrance to Blyth Harbour. The West Pier stretches over 400 metres out to sea and the worn wooden planks and metal railings serve as perfect leading lines to the end of the pier (pictured above). The East Pier is inaccessible, however it's still a good subject when shot across the water from the beach or West Pier, with the lighthouse at the end adding interest. Both of these compositions can be captured at any tide height, although the scene looking along the West Pier is cleaner when the tide is in and it's surrounded by water.

Finally, just to the south of the promenade are three long wooden groynes in a fairly good state of repair (pictured below). To capture the waves whooshing around the ends, or reflections in the wet sand, aim for an hour or two before low tide.

There's a tide station at Blyth, so use those tide times to plan your visit. South Beach is a perfect sunrise location, but equally good with stormy skies and for sunset if there's some colour in the clouds.

» How to get there

From the A189 at Cramlington, take the A1061 to Blyth and at the roundabout by the sea take the second exit signed "Beach". If you're coming from Seaton Sluice on the A193, it's the third exit on the roundabout. You'll find a large car park on your right (free). There's also another small car park 300 metres further along near the bandstand (also free). The jetty and beach huts are in front of the main car park, the groynes are to the south and the pipe and pier are to the north — see the map on page 50 for the exact locations.

» Grid references

NZ 320 795 for the main car park (postcode NE24 3PL), NZ 320 799 for the small car park.

27 SEATON SLUICE

This small village lies at the mouth of the Seaton Burn and has a tiny traditional walled harbour dating back to the 1600s. There are tall ladders scattered along the walls and plenty of small fishing boats moored up, creating a very charming seaside scene. You can walk all the way around it so there are a wealth of different angles to investigate and it's generally more attractive when full, so aim for high tide if you can.

Protecting the harbour entrance is an unusual groyne, braced with large wooden struts on the beachward side and with a marker post at the end. This looks fabulous with the sea swirling around the struts (pictured on the right) and is best around an hour either side of high tide.

Next to the harbour is Rocky Island – a small grass-covered island with a platform of rocks surrounding it. The rocks provide endless opportunities for long-exposure seascapes and there's an old watch house on the eastern edge that also makes a pleasing scene when combined with the nearby fence as a leading line.

Just to the south of Rocky Island is Collywell Bay and another excellent subject – a sea stack called Charlie's Garden (pictured below). Although it's not the largest sea stack in the world it is very striking when completely surrounded by water, so it's an

ideal location around high tide. The bay has a narrow pebble beach and plenty of rocks for foreground, including a very attractive outcrop of sandstone that's also great for abstract close-ups, with swirls of muted pinks, purples and yellows.

All the locations at Seaton Sluice are suitable for both sunrise and sunset, apart from the harbour, which is better at sunset. The beach in Collywell Bay and the rocks around Rocky Island are both backed by high cliffs, so I wouldn't recommend shooting at these places on a rising tide (the nearest tide station is Blyth). You can safely shoot Charlie's Garden from the path down to the beach at the height of high tide though, and the view is still great.

» How to get there

Seaton Sluice is on the A193 between Blyth and Whitley Bay. There's a free car park at the north end of the village, just off the roundabout on the main road, but if you turn off the A193 into the village you'll find plenty of roadside parking too. See the map on page 51 for the locations of the groyne, harbour, Rocky Island and Charlie's Garden. The beach in front of Charlie's Garden is accessed from a steep paved path that leads down from the road.

» Grid references

NZ 332 771 for the car park, NZ 336 769 for the groyne, NZ 340 766 for Charlie's Garden, postcode for the village for Satnav is NE26 4QZ.

28 ST MARY'S LIGHTHOUSE

Built in 1898 this elegant lighthouse dominates the tiny island of St Mary's, which lies just to the north

of Whitley Bay and is linked to the mainland by a short tidal causeway. It's arguably the most popular photography location on this stretch of coast, but for very good reason – it's a stunning setting surrounded by fantastic geology and there are numerous viewpoints to explore whatever the tide height.

One of the best viewpoints is from the start of the causeway, using it as a leading line to the lighthouse (pictured on the left). This scene is superb when the tide is in and the causeway is covered by the sea (it's submerged for approximately two hours either side of high tide). A bit of wave action adds drama to the composition and the small flight of steps down onto the shore can also be included for extra foreground interest.

Just to the left of the causeway is a small sandy beach with a scattering of large rocks and a short line of tall wooden posts that are the remains of a long-gone jetty. At the end of the beach there's also an interesting platform of cracked bedrock that makes fantastic foreground (pictured on the next page). This is more attractive when the tide is in, as there's a clean separation between the rocks and lighthouse. With so much variety in this area it's a popular choice for many.

When the tide is out and the island is accessible even more potential is revealed. There's an expanse of rocks surrounding the lighthouse with plenty of ledges and rockpools to explore for compositions – reflections of the lighthouse in rockpools work particularly well, as do using ripples in the sand as leading lines. Behind the lighthouse you'll discover a rangefinder – a large concrete pillar built in 1914 to calibrate coastal defence guns. This is a great subject in its own right with the waves washing around it. Also, if you're lucky you may spot some grey seals – these can sometimes be seen resting on the rocks, especially during spring and early summer.

Finally, to the northwest of the island at Old Hartley is a long wave-cut platform of sandstone rock. Much of the rock is jointed into large blocks, creating some fantastic patterns and giving you endless foreground to choose from with the lighthouse on the horizon in the background. Different ledges are exposed at different tide heights, but within two hours of high tide is generally good. This isn't a place where you want to be caught out by rising water levels though, as the shore is backed by very high cliffs and can be completely covered at high tide, so if the tide is coming in keep a watchful eye on it at all times, but ideally visit on a falling tide.

You can get colourful skies and wonderful rich side lighting on the lighthouse at both sunrise and sunset, but during the day can be just as productive if there are interesting conditions. Having said that, the island is very popular with day-trippers, so going early or late has the added benefit of being quieter. The island is roughly equidistant from Blyth and North Shields tide stations, so use times from either to plan your visit.

» How to get there

St Mary's Island is just off the A193 between Seaton Sluice and Whitley Bay. The turning for it is on a sharp bend at the northern end of Whitley Bay, signed "St Mary's Island". Continue to the end of the road and just before the causeway you will find a large car park on the left (Pay & Display). If you're going onto the island make sure you know when the last safe crossing time for the causeway is – handily, these are listed on a notice board at the car park. For Old Hartley, take the A193 north for about a mile and at the roundabout by the Delavel Arms pub take the exit towards the sea. Follow the road straight down and you'll find a small free car park at the bottom. Follow the path out of the car park towards St Mary's and after about 100 metres you'll find some steps just off the main path that lead down onto the shore.

» Grid references

NZ 351 751 for St Mary's Island Car Park (postcode NE26 4RS), NZ 344 757 for Old Hartley (nearest postcode NE26 4RL).

29 CULLERCOATS

The small semi-circular bay at Cullercoats has a sandy beach backed by cliffs and two protective piers jutting out on either side. Of the two piers, the North Pier is the most photogenic, as it's slightly curved and has a cobbled stone surface. Around high tide the incoming waves roll over the pier and flow off the other side, creating fantastic opportunities for long-exposures, especially at sunrise. You can shoot it from height by the watchtower on the road or from the pier itself (don't walk along it if the waves are coming over though). On the headland at the southern side of the bay is Saddle Rocks, which has a small sea arch (pictured above). To get a decent view of it you do have to venture onto the cliffs, which is a little bit precarious. It looks most attractive within two hours of high tide when there's water under the arch (North Shields is the closest tide station).

» How to get there

Cullercoats is between Whitley Bay and Tynemouth. The roadside parking on the seafront is mostly for permit holders only, so the best place to park is Front Street Car Park (free), which is roughly opposite the Queen's Head pub. If there's no space, there's another free car park on Belle Vue Street – at the mini-roundabout turn into the town and take the first right turn you see.

» Grid references

NZ 364 714 for the North Pier, NZ 366 711 for Saddle Rocks (postcode for parking NE30 4QB).

30 TYNEMOUTH

With a pretty Victorian seafront, this seaside town has a rather charming feel to it. As the name suggests, it lies at the mouth of the River Tyne, and has a dramatic headland guarded by sheer cliffs, as well as a couple of lovely sandy beaches.

Perched on the headland are the ruins of Tynemouth Priory, which has a long and varied history dating back to the 11th century. The site is actually a hotchpotch of old World War II defences, military buildings and the remains of Tynemouth Castle, but it's the priory with its elegant windows and arches that's the main photographic attraction. There's also a very atmospheric graveyard beside the ruins with some elaborately inscribed and unusually weathered headstones. If you enjoy interior architecture make sure you visit the Percy Chapel too – it has an ornate vaulted ceiling and some beautiful stained-glass windows.

Jutting out from the headland is the massive North Pier, one of two breakwaters that protect the port entrance, and there are numerous compositions to explore around it. You can stroll along the pier to investigate the views of the lighthouse at the end, but only during daylight hours as the gates are closed at night (and in bad weather). At the start of the pier is a small viewing platform, which is a safe place to shoot waves crashing into the pier in stormy weather (shown below),

although you can still get very wet here if you don't keep an eye on the incoming waves. A flight of stone steps lead down from the platform to the shore, giving you a totally different perspective with the pier leading out into the sea on the right of the frame. You'll find plenty of rocks for foreground, but avoid the peak of high tide as it's backed by very high cliffs and the steps are the only way out (the closest tide station to here is North Shields). The shore to the east of the pier, known as Prior's Haven, has views to both North and South Piers and can also be productive.

To the north of the pier and priory are two sandy bays – King Edward's Bay (also known as Short Sands) and Longsands. There's a good view from the northern side of King Edward's Bay, looking southeast across it to the pier

and the priory ruins on the top of the cliffs. This looks attractive from the beach, where you'll find plenty of rocks to choose from for foreground (pictured on the next page), but also from a higher vantage point on the road. It's a good location for sunrise, but although the ruins will be lit by the late evening Sun, the bay is heavily shaded at this time of day.

From the southern end of Longsands there's a delightful view along the beach towards Cullercoats, with St George's Church providing a compelling focal point (pictured above). There's also an old outdoor swimming pool at this end that has potential and around low tide a few rocks are exposed in the middle of the beach, which add interest to compositions looking south. Sunrise is a terrific time to visit as the bay is bathed in warm

light. Longsands is very popular with locals and tourists alike, so go early or late to avoid the crowds. It's also one of the finest surf spots on the northeast coast, so take a long lens if you want to try some action shots.

» How to get there

There are multiple places to park in Tynemouth. I've labelled them on the map on page 53, but will give you the closest one for each location. For the priory, the closest parking is on Front Street, which is the main street of pubs and shops, and has free parking down the middle. The priory is run by English Heritage and there's an entrance fee to go inside – see www.english-heritage.org.uk for ticket prices and opening times.

For the pier, there's a handy free car park near Tynemouth Sailing Club. To get to it take the turning by the priory, next to the small clocktower, and you'll find it down the hill on the right-hand side. If that's full, there's another car park straight ahead on the point (Pay & Display). For King Edward's Bay and Longsands you'll find roadside parking all along the seafront, which is mainly Pay & Display.

» Grid references

NZ 373 694 for the priory (postcode for Front Street parking NE30 4BT), NZ 374 693 for the pier (nearest postcode for the car park is NE30 4DB), NZ 372 699 for King Edward's Bay view, NZ 370 699 for Longsands view.

4 Castles &
Countryside

SECTION

Many photographers overlook the countryside in favour of the coast, but it has plenty to offer, with waterfalls, heather moorlands, ancient woodland, castles and other historical sites scattered around the county. It would take an entire book to cover this vast area in detail, so in this section I've given you a taster of the best on offer (and I've squeezed in a couple of extra suggestions at the back of the book too – see page 111.)

The majority of the countryside, especially in the east and south, is gently rolling farmland that's easy walking and particularly delightful in the summer when the different crops create a patchwork of coloured fields. Running down the western side of the county, from Wooler in the north to Hadrian's Wall in the south, is Northumberland National Park. It covers over 400 square miles and has a variety of different landscapes.

At the northern end of the park are the mighty Cheviot Hills. These distinctive rounded hills can be seen from many places in Northumberland, but up-close are wild and rugged. Many of the valleys that lead into the Cheviots are interesting to explore, such as College Valley, Breamish Valley and Harthope Valley. And Upper Coquetdale (pronounced ko-ket-dale) on the southern fringe is also beautiful. For those of you wanting a challenging walk in the Cheviots I'd recommend Windy Gyle, but for the less energetic a drive up any of these valleys (especially Upper Coquetdale) can be photographically rewarding, although be aware that many of the roads are single-track.

The southern Cheviots include the Otterburn Ranges – a huge area of moorland owned by the Ministry of Defence and used for military training. Access is prohibited when there's live firing (marked by red flags flying at the entry points), but is accessible at all other times.

Although the Cheviots have some heather moorland, Coquetdale is a great place to shoot the spectacular colours in late summer – the Simonside Hills near Rothbury being one of the best places to go.

Finally, at the southwestern corner of Northumberland is Kielder Water and Kielder Forest Park. Due to being relatively flat, Kielder is uninspiring for vistas, but it does have plenty of coniferous woodland if you enjoy this type of inner landscape. It's a huge area with many walking trails, but for starters I'd suggest the Hindhope Linn trail.

SECTION 4: CASTLES & COUNTRYSIDE

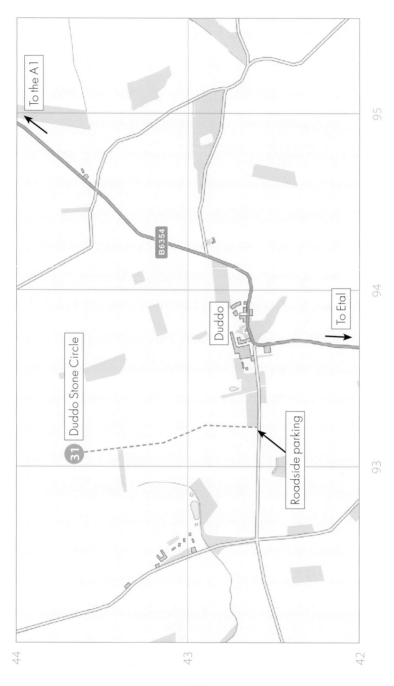

To the A1

B6354

Duddo

To Etal

31 Duddo Stone Circle

Roadside parking

95

94

93

44

43

42

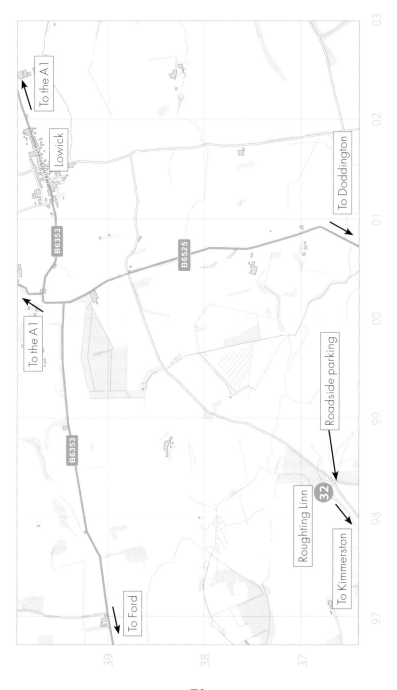

To the A1

Lowick

To Doddington

B6353

B6525

To the A1

B6353

Roadside parking

32

Roughting Linn

To Kimmerston

To Ford

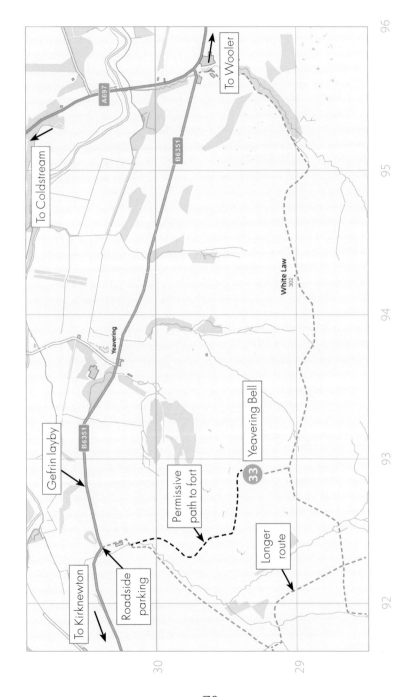

To Wooler

To Coldstream

A697

B6351

White Law
302

Yeavering

Yeavering Bell

Gefrin layby

B6351

Permissive
path to fort

33

Longer
route

To Kirknewton

Roadside
parking

30

29

96

95

94

93

92

73

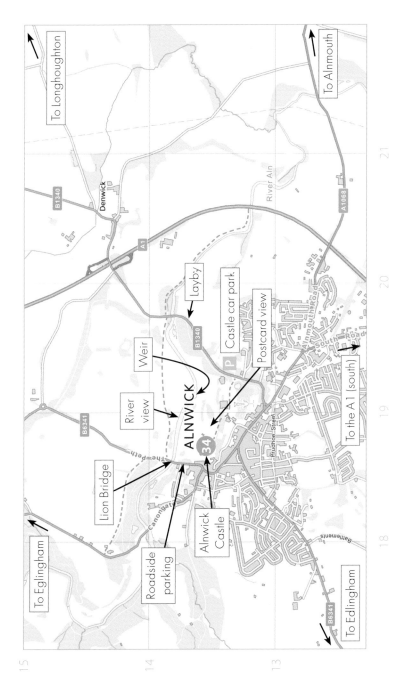

To Longhoughton

To Alnmouth

B1340

Denwick

A1

River Aln

A1068

21

20

Layby

Castle car park

Postcard view

B1340

P

Weir

River view

ALNWICK

Threepeth

34

To the A1 (south)

South Road

Alnmouth Road

Prudhoe Street

Lion Bridge

Canongate

Roadside parking

Alnwick Castle

Battlements

To Eglingham

B6341

B6341

To Edlingham

15

14

13

18

19

74

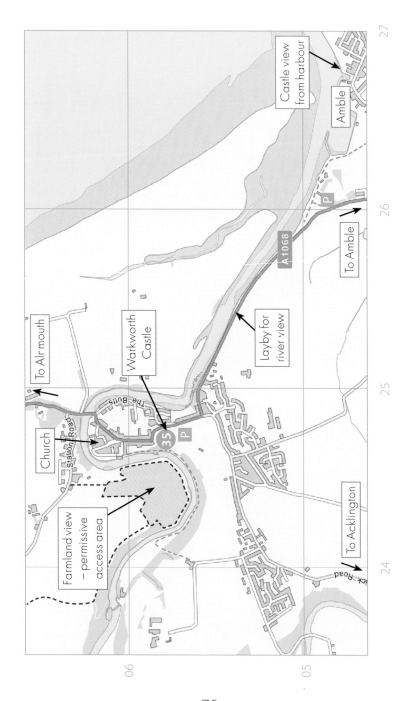

Castle view from harbour

Amble

To Amble

A1068

Layby for river view

To Alnmouth

Warkworth Castle

The Butts

Station Road

Church

Farmland view – permissive access area

To Acklington

ck Road

75

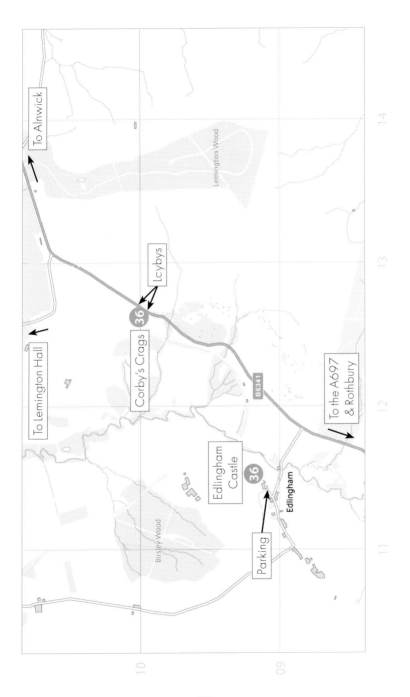

To Alnwick

Lemington Wood

Lcybys

To Lemington Hall

36

Corby's Crags

B6341

To the A697
& Rothbury

Edlingham
Castle

36

Edlingham

Birsley Wood

Parking

14

13

12

11

10

09

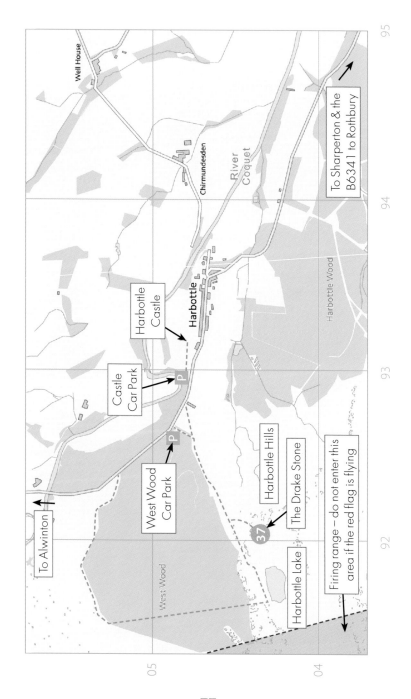

Well House

Chirmundesden

River Coquet

To Sharperton & the
B6341 to Rothbury

Harbottle
Castle

Harbottle

Harbottle Wood

Castle
Car Park

West Wood
Car Park

Harbottle Hills

The Drake Stone

37

To Alwinton

West Wood

Harbottle Lake

Firing range – do not enter this
area if the red flag is flying

95

94

93

92

05

04

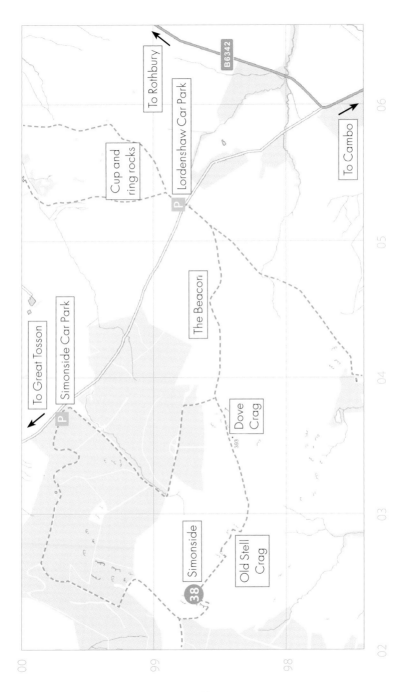

To Rothbury

B6342

Cup and ring rocks

Lordenshaw Car Park

To Cambo

To Great Tosson

Simonside Car Park

The Beacon

Dove Crag

Simonside

Old Stell Crag

393

38

00

99

98

06

05

04

03

02

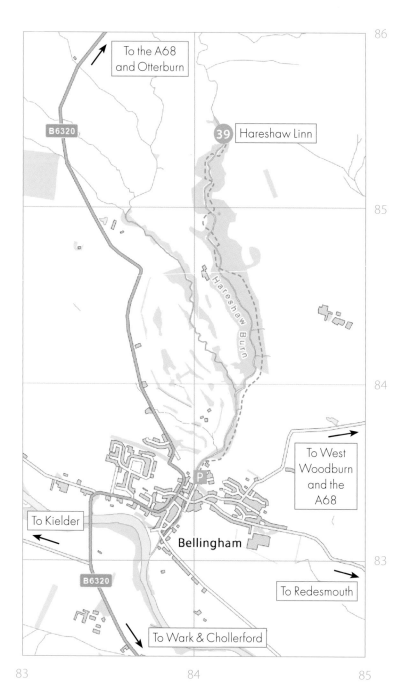

To the A68
and Otterburn

B6320

39 Hareshaw Linn

Hareshaw Burn

To West
Woodburn
and the
A68

P

To Kielder

Bellingham

B6320

To Redesmouth

To Wark & Chollerford

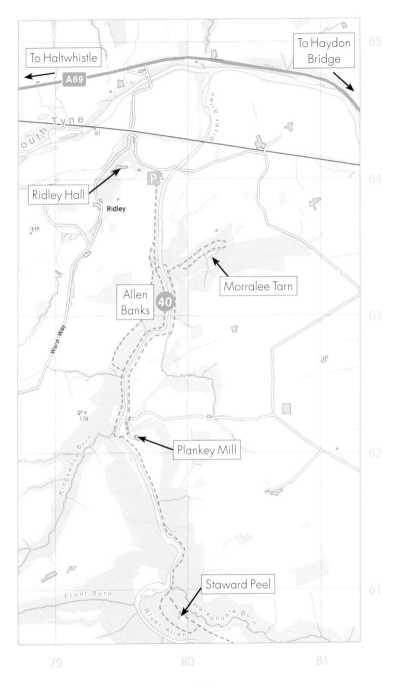

To Haltwhistle

A69

To Haydon Bridge

Ridley Hall

Ridley

South Tyne

River Allen

Morralee Tarn

Allen Banks

40

Ward Way

Kingswood Burn

Plankey Mill

Staward Peel

Front Burn

Harsondale Burn

River Allen

65

64

63

62

61

79

80

81

31 DUDDO STONE CIRCLE

This small stone circle is around 4000 years old and consists of five sandstone monoliths that have been heavily weathered over the years. It sits atop a low hill with panoramic views of the surrounding countryside, but due to its position there's very little background, so you do need good light or an interesting sky to get a decent photo here. Since you can shoot it from any direction it's suitable for both sunrise and sunset. It's particularly attractive in early summer when the crops are at their highest, as the path up the hill through the field makes a good leading line.

» How to get there

From the A1 just south of Berwick-Upon-Tweed, take the B6354 towards Duddo and Etal. When you reach Duddo village take the right turn signposted "Tiptoe, Shellacres" and "Stone Circle". About 500 metres down this lane you'll find a gateway on your right with a "Stone Circle" sign by it. Park on the verge here, taking care not to block the gateway. Go through the gate and follow the permissive path through the fields to the circle. It takes about 20 minutes and can be quite muddy after rain.

» Grid references

NT 932 426 for parking, NT 931 437 for the circle (nearest postcode for satnav TD15 2PS).

32 ROUGHTING LINN

This delightful waterfall is situated in a patch of woodland near the villages of Lowick and Ford. It cascades over a sandstone cliff into a small gorge and has a single drop of around 7 metres. The gorge is filled with moss-covered rocks, ferns and fallen tree branches, giving it a slightly mystical feel. An overcast day is best, with normal to low water levels if possible, and wellies are very handy here for getting into a good position. As for time of year, I'd recommend going in the summer when the surrounding foliage is at its greenest.

» How to get there

From the A1 about 1½ miles south of the Holy Island turn-off, take the B6353 towards Lowick and Fenwick. Continue through the village of Lowick and turn left at the T-junction. After two thirds of a mile look out for a tiny crossroads with a small house on the left. Turn right here onto a narrow lane. Follow the lane for two miles and when you get to a small left-hand turn park on the verge. Walk down the track opposite the turning, signed "Roughting Linn Farm". After roughly 100 metres there's a tiny path on the left (if you can hear the waterfall below you, you've gone past it). Follow this path down and round to the right to the foot of the waterfall. It only takes about 5 minutes but the descent is steep and tricky underfoot.

» Grid references

NT 984 366 for parking (nearest postcode TD15 2QF), NT 982 368 for the waterfall.

33 YEAVERING BELL

At the top of this rounded hill are the remains of a prehistoric hillfort, dating back around 2500 years. The summit itself is rather featureless, however the tumbled boundary wall that encircles it more than makes up for this. The band of lichen-covered stones makes fine foreground for the expansive panoramic views, which range from patchwork farmland in the north to rolling moorland in the south. It's most attractive in summer and with 360° views is suitable from dawn to dusk.

» How to get there

From Wooler take the A697 to Coldstream. After nearly 3 miles turn left to Yeavering and Kirknewton. After another 2 miles look out for a small layby on the right for "Gefrin" (a minor historical site). Just after this you'll find a farm track on the left. Park on the verge here, making sure you don't block the track or any gateways (if there's no room park in the Gefrin layby). Walk up the track, past the cottages and turn left after the barn onto the permissive path. Follow the marker posts across the fields – the path bears right first, then left after the wall and up the hill. It takes about 40 minutes and is very steep. (For a longer but slightly gentler route, continue along the farm track for ¾ of a mile and turn left after a cattlegrid onto St Cuthbert's Way, then left again after half a mile to come up the back of the hill.)

» Grid references

NT 924 304 for roadside parking (postcode NE71 6HF), NT 928 293 for the summit.

34 ALNWICK CASTLE

With magnificent turrets, cobbled courtyards and plush interiors this well-preserved castle is one of the most impressive in the North. While photography isn't allowed in the lavish state rooms, there's still a huge variety of scenes and details to shoot within the walls. Just before the main entrance gates there's also a picture-postcard view of the outside, which is best in April when the lawn is covered in daffodils. However, the most inspiring view is from the other side of the River Aln, with the castle reflected in the water (pictured above). This is best from the banking near Lion Bridge and

there are plenty of rushes and reeds for foreground, as well as a weir further along. I prefer this viewpoint at sunrise, with the warm morning light bathing the landscape, but it also works well at sunset. And you're in for a treat if it's frosty or there's a bit of mist lingering on the river. There's also an interesting composition from Lion Bridge itself, with the stone lion statue on the bridge parapet positioned in front of the castle.

» How to get there

From the A1 it's easiest to take the northern exit to Alnwick (signed "Alnwick Garden & Castle") rather than the southern one. For the main castle car park, at the A1 exit turn onto the B1340 to Alnwick and you'll find it on the left after a mile (£3 all day). Disabled parking is on the right a little further along the road. See www.alnwickcastle.com for opening times and ticket prices. You don't need a ticket for the postcard view of the outside. N.B. the castle is closed in winter, usually from November to the end of March. For the river view, it's quicker to park near Lion Bridge. Once you've left the A1 and turned onto the B1340, turn immediately right towards Eglingham (if you're coming from the south you almost

go straight across at the end of the A1 slip road). Follow the road along and turn left at the roundabout at the end. The castle comes into view as you head down the hill – go over the bridge and park on the side of the road. Walk back over the bridge and there's a gate onto the public footpath by the river on the right.

» Grid references

NU 188 138 for the river view (Lion Bridge nearest postcode NE66 1JQ), postcode for the castle car park NE66 1YU.

35 WARKWORTH CASTLE

The well-preserved remains of this medieval castle tower high above the quaint village of Warkworth, which lies just a mile or so from the coast in a loop of the River Coquet. There's plenty to shoot inside the ruins, but you can also walk around the outside at any time of day or night to take in the grand gatehouse, impressive towers and imposing keep. April is a superb time to visit as the hilltop is carpeted in daffodils. For a wider view, one of the best places is from the fields of Hermitage Farm to the west of the castle, on the other side of the river (pictured on the right). From here you can capture the castle poking out above the

treetops, which is best in summer when the landscape is a luscious green, but it's also attractive with frost or snow in winter. As you're looking east it's suitable for sunrise, but the late evening light catches the castle walls too. There's also a pleasing longer view of the castle from the River Coquet to the east of the village. This is particularly good if the water is still and the scene is reflected in the estuary. Another good location for long views up the estuary is Amble Harbour, especially at sunset, although you will need a long lens to fill the frame with the castle from here.

» How to get there

The castle is just off the A1068 on the southern side of the village. It has a pay & display car park

right next to it and the cost is deducted from the ticket price if you go inside the castle. See www.english-heritage.org.uk for ticket prices and opening times. The car park is usually closed when the castle is closed, so if you're visiting out-of-hours park on the main street in the village. There's also free parking on the road in front of the church and along the river behind the church. For the farmland view, drive out of the village towards Alnmouth and after you cross the bridge take the first left turn you come to, signposted "Shilbottle". Continue up the lane and park sensibly on the side of the road somewhere before the national speed limit sign (take care not to block any driveways). Between the last two houses on the left you'll find a small path. Follow this along, bearing right when it opens out a little, and you'll find a gate into a large field with views of the castle. This land is permissive access, so please be considerate. It takes about 6 minutes and the path and field can be quite muddy. Please note that there's no access from Hermitage Farm itself – only use the permissive path. For the longer river view, take the A1068 from the castle towards Amble and you'll find a layby next to the river after roughly half a mile.

» Grid references

NU 247 057 for the castle car park (postcode NE65 0UJ), NU 244 059 for the farmland view, NU 254 054 for the river view.

36 EDLINGHAM

The little village of Edlingham lies between Alnwick and Rothbury and has two sites of photographic interest I'd recommend. The first is Edlingham Castle, which is a small fortified manor house built in the 1300s, although only the tower remains largely intact. The ruins looks fantastic in the late evening light or with dramatic clouds and processed into black and white. The second location is Corby's Crags, to the northeast of the village. From this high vantage point you get wide views over the surrounding countryside to the Cheviots in the distance (pictured above). A long lens is handy here for picking out details such as the castle. It's a good spot for sunset and there's a scattering of rocks and a lone bench for foreground.

» How to get there

The village is just off the B6341, 6 miles from Alnwick and 7 miles from Rothbury. For the castle, turn into the village (which is a right turn if you're coming from Alnwick and a left if you're coming from Rothbury). Take the next right turn you come to, signposted "Castle & 11th c. Church" and park beside the church. Go through the gate next to the church and walk down the field to the castle. (There's no entry fee.) For Corby's Crags, go back to the B6341 and turn left towards Alnwick. After 1 mile you'll find two small laybys on the left, right on the edge of the crags.

» Grid references

NU 114 091 for castle parking (nearest postcode NE66 2BN), NU 126 099 for Corby's Crags.

37 HARBOTTLE HILLS

Harbottle is a tiny village in the Upper Coquet Valley, to the west of Rothbury. The Harbottle Hills lie to the south of the village and are littered with an assortment of sandstone boulders, including an enormous erratic called the Drake Stone. The hillside is carpeted in heather and the extensive views back down to the village and the remains of Harbottle Castle are fantastic. There are endless compositions to explore and also a few small rowan trees scattered around for extra interest. It's superb in late summer when the heather is in bloom, but early autumn is also a great time to visit as the rowan trees are bursting with bright red berries.

» How to get there

From Rothbury take the B6341 towards Otterburn. After four miles turn right to Harbottle. When you reach the village continue through it and on the other side you'll find West Wood Car Park on the left (free). Follow the track out of the car park signposted "Drakestone" and after 100 metres go through the gate on the left. (Don't worry if the red MOD flag is flying here – this location is outside the firing range, just don't go past the lake). Follow the path up the hill and at the fork near the top take the path on the left. It takes about 20 minutes and although it isn't too steep it is quite uneven underfoot. If you also want to visit the ruins of Harbottle Castle there's a small car park for it (free – see the map on page 77 for the location) and no entrance fee.

» Grid references

NT 926 049 for West Wood Car Park (postcode NE65 7BB), NT 921 044 for the Drake Stone.

on the left). Next along the route is Old Stell Crag, which is a jumble of giant sandstone boulders with many angles to explore. When you finally reach Simonside the crags drop off sharply below you, giving way to a spectacular view over the patchwork fields of Coquetdale with the Cheviot Hills in the distance (shown on the right). The path is paved along much of the route and is a good subject in its own right as it winds across the moorland. Although it's a great location year-round the scenery is transformed in late summer when the expanse of heather turns various hues of purple.

38 SIMONSIDE

To the south of Rothbury lie the Simonside Hills – a long sandstone escarpment topped by a range of low peaks. The two-mile ridge walk to the summit of Simonside itself is one of the finest in Northumberland and has a lot to offer photographically. Starting from the east the first high point you reach is The Beacon, where you'll find a circular cairn and the views begin to open out. Things begin to get really interesting at the next crag along, Dove Crag, which has a beautifully weathered outcrop of rock and interesting views west to Simonside (pictured

» **How to get there**

From Rothbury take the B6342 towards Hexham and Cambo. After 3 miles take the right turn to Simonside, which is on a sharp left-hand bend and signposted with a brown sign. Continue along the single-track lane and after you emerge from the woods you'll find Lordenshaw car park on the right (free). Cross the road and follow the obvious path up the hill, bearing right at the first fork. This clear path leads all the way along the ridge to Simonside, which takes about an hour. If the car park is full, there's another one in the forest just over a mile further down the lane (called Simonside car park – also free). From here, follow the red waymarked trail through the wood up onto the ridge. Also, if you've got some spare time and are interested in prehistoric rock art, you'll find a scattering of rocks with cup and ring markings on the moorland beside Lordenshaw car park.

» Grid references

NZ 053 988 for Lordenshaw car park (nearest postcode NE61 4PU), NZ 037 997 for Simonside car park, NZ 024 987 for Simonside summit.

39 HARESHAW LINN

At the top of a wooded gorge, just to the north of the village of Bellingham, Hareshaw Burn plunges over dramatic sandstone cliffs, creating this stunning 10-metre high cascading waterfall. There's plenty of foreground to explore and while wellies aren't essential here they are quite useful. There are also many opportunities on the upper reaches of the river to do long-exposure shots, with numerous small cascades and bridges criss-crossing the river. The ideal time to visit is on an overcast day, with normal to low water levels, and it's most attractive in summer and autumn when the surrounding deciduous woodland is brimming with rich colours.

» How to get there

From the main street in Bellingham, take the turning signposted "West Woodburn, Redesmouth" (a right turn if you're coming from Kielder or Chollerford, a left turn if coming from the A68 on the B6320). Take the next left turn you come to and you'll find the car park just up this lane on the left (free). If you're coming from the A68 at West Woodburn, turn right just before the main street, opposite the garage. Follow the path out of the back of the car park all the way to the waterfall. It's 1½ miles and takes about 40 minutes. The path is well maintained, but can be muddy in places and has a few steep sections.

» Grid references

NY 840 835 for the car park (NE48 2BZ), NY 842 854 for the waterfall.

40 ALLEN BANKS

Tucked away to the southwest of Haydon Bridge is Allen Banks – a beautiful wooded gorge carved out by the River Allen. It's a great location for inner landscapes and long-exposure river scenes, and there are a choice of waymarked paths along the river and through the ancient woodland. The area between the car park and Plankey Mill is the most photogenic and fairly easy going, but if you want to extend your walk I'd suggest Morralee Tarn on the eastern side of the woods (the other option is a high point called Staward Peel, but the views are mostly obscured by trees). Spring is a great time to visit to investigate the bluebells and wild garlic, however autumn is the highlight of the year as the colours are simply superb.

» How to get there

From the A69 three miles west of Haydon Bridge, take the turning signposted with a brown sign to "Allen Banks & Staward Gorge" (it's a left if you're coming from Haydon Bridge, a right if you're coming from Haltwhistle). After you pass under a railway bridge turn left and you'll find a car park quarter of a mile along the road on the right (National Trust, Pay & Display). The routes of the waymarked paths are shown on a display board at the car park *.

» Grid references

NY 798 640 for the car park (nearest postcode NE47 7BP).

* At the time of going to print, some paths at Allen Banks are closed due to storm damage, but alternative routes are in place. See www.nationaltrust.org.uk/allen-banks-and-staward-gorge for details.

5 Hadrian's Wall

Stretching 73 miles from coast to coast this defensive wall was built by the order of Emperor Hadrian in 122 AD to protect the northern border of the Roman Empire. The wall varied in height, width and construction method along its length and roughly every five Roman miles there was a large fort hosting garrisons of infantry and cavalry. Furthermore, every Roman mile a small fort called a milecastle was built, with two turrets between each milecastle for observation and signalling. These were named with a numbering system from east to west, e.g. Milecastle 39.

The central section of the wall, near the border of Northumberland and Cumbria, is the most well preserved and undoubtedly the most photogenic as the wall snakes and twists along a whinstone ridge. The Romans used the ridge to their advantage as a natural defence, building the wall directly along the series of high crags and creating some truly striking scenes in the process. The wall runs roughly east to west, making it suitable for both sunrise and sunset, although as the wall zigzags so much its a good idea to check the seasonal variations in the direction of the Sun for your chosen location (see page 118 for more on this). I haven't specified the best time of year to visit each location in the following pages as Hadrian's Wall is wonderful in all seasons – the surrounding farmland is most verdant in the spring and summer, but misty autumn mornings bring added photographic potential, as does frost and snow in the winter.

A continuous footpath runs the length of the wall and this is accessed from the B6318, known locally as the military road. It runs roughly parallel to the wall on the southern side and can be easily reached from many points along the A69, such as Haltwhistle or Greenhead. The car parks along the military road are all Pay & Display (at the time of writing, £4 for the day), but tickets are transferable between the car parks. If you intend to visit the wall quite a few times it's worth getting an annual pass from the visitor centre at Walltown or Once Brewed (£20). From the end of March to the end of September the Hadrian's Wall Bus runs between the various car parks along the B6318, providing a very handy way to do one-way walks along the wall. Hadrian's Wall is a UNESCO World Heritage Site so please help to conserve it by refraining from walking or climbing on it. N.B. only locations 42, 44 and 50 are accessible by wheelchair.

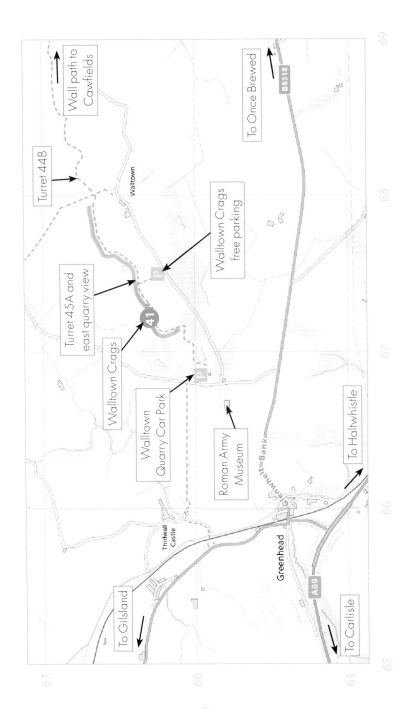

Wall path to Cawfields

Turret 44B

Walltown

Turret 45A and east quarry view

Walltown Crags free parking

Walltown Crags

Walltown Quarry Car Park

Roman Army Museum

To Once Brewed

B6318

Glenwhelt Bank

Greenhead

Thirlwall Castle

To Gilsland

To Haltwhistle

A69

To Carlisle

69

68

67

66

65

67

66

65

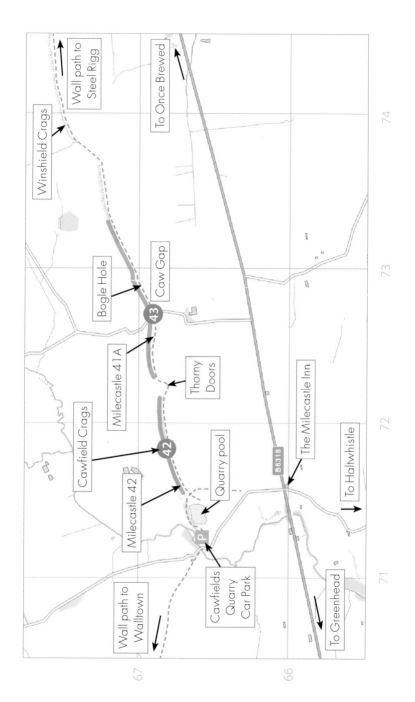

Winshield Crags

Wall path to
Steel Rigg

To Once Brewed

Bogle Hole

Caw Gap

43

Milecastle 41 A

Thorny
Doors

Cawfield Crags

42

Milecastle 42

Quarry pool

The Milecastle Inn

To Halthwhistle

B6318

Cawfields Quarry
Car Park

P

Wall path to
Walltown

To Greenhead

67

66

74

73

72

71

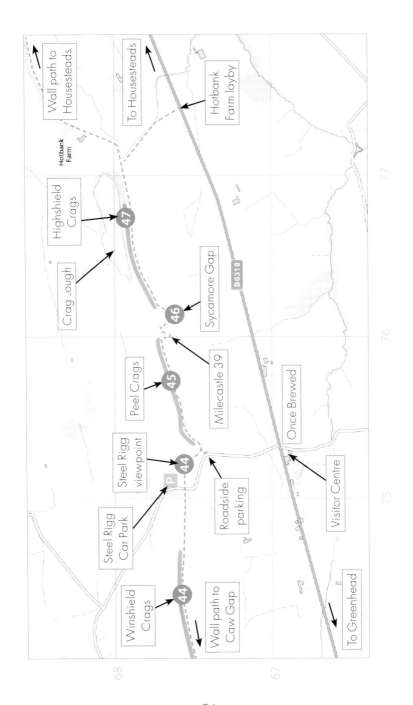

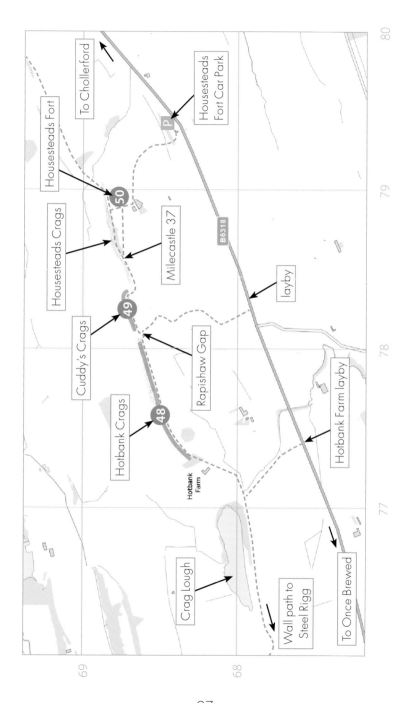

To Chollerford

Housesteads Fort Car Park

Housesteads Fort

Housesteads Crags

Milecastle 37

Cuddy's Crags

B6318

layby

Rapishaw Gap

Hotbank Crags

Hotbank Farm layby

Hotbank Farm

Crag Lough

Wall path to Steel Rigg

To Once Brewed

48
49
50

P

41 WALLTOWN CRAGS

The impressive whinstone cliffs of Walltown Crags were quarried extensively during Victorian times, mainly for road building stone, and although the area has been re-landscaped since the quarry closed in the 1970s signs of the area's industrial past, such as small quarry pools, are still visible. Despite various parts of Hadrian's Wall being destroyed by the quarrying, at the western end of the crags is one of the finest sections on the entire wall (shown on the next page). This 400-metre long stretch undulates along the top of the ridge and winds around lichen-covered rocky outcrops,

creating numerous compositions to explore. The main path runs along the southern side of the wall, but with care you can also walk along the northern side. With views in all directions and on both sides of the wall it's suitable at any time of day. There are also plenty of lone trees along the crags, which can add interest to compositions and look particularly atmospheric on misty mornings. One of the most popular views at this location is looking east along the crags over the eastern quarry (shown above). This is generally best in the late evening light of the summer months when the north-facing crags are illuminated, but is still suitable for sunrise as you're looking east. You can venture further east from this point if you like, but the wall largely disappears until you get to Cawfields. However, if you do want to stretch your legs you'll find a good view back over the east quarry from further along the Hadrian's Wall path, and there's also a nice view west over Turret 44B from the next crags along (called Mucklebank Crags).

» How to get there

From the B6318 about half a mile east of Greenhead, take the turning signposted "Walltown Quarry, Walltown Crags". Take the next right turn you come to, opposite the Roman Army Museum, signposted "Walltown Crags". Half a mile along this single-track lane you'll find a free parking area on the left (N.B. there are few passing places along the lane). It's a couple of minutes' walk straight up the field to the wall. Turn right for the quarry view and left for the attractive stretch of wall. If the parking area is full, park at Walltown Quarry, which is the next right after the Roman Army Museum (Pay & Display). Follow either path past the picnic area to the crags and turn left onto the wall path, following it up onto the top of the crags. It takes about 20 minutes to get to the east quarry view.

» Grid references

NY 675 662 for Walltown Crags free parking (nearest postcode CA8 7JD), NY 668 659 for Walltown Quarry car park (nearest postcode CA8 7JB), NY 674 663 for the quarry view.

42 CAWFIELDS

Cawfields is another former quarry, with dramatic whinstone cliffs and a large tranquil pool formed from the abandoned pit. When the wind is low and the sheer cliffs are reflected in the still water it creates a fantastic scene. This view is suitable for both sunrise (when the crags are silhouetted) and in the late evening (when they'll be lit). To the east of the quarry is an impressive stretch of Hadrian's Wall running along Cawfield Crags. It's well worth venturing up to explore the views here, especially the first section where you're treated to a spectacular vista over Milecastle 42 back towards the quarry crags and pool (pictured above).

Again, this works well at sunrise, when you get rich sidelighting on the wall, as well as at sunset.

» How to get there

From the B6318 about 2½ miles west of Once Brewed, take the turning opposite the Milecastle Inn, signposted "Cawfields". Just along this road you'll find a car park on the right (Pay & Display). The quarry pool is in front of the car park. For the crags, follow the path around the pool and bear right onto the wall path. It takes 5 minutes to get to Milecastle 42.

» Grid references

NY 713 666 for the car park and quarry pool (nearest postcode NE49 9PJ), NY 716 667 for the milecastle view.

43 CAW GAP

This gap in the crags along Hadrian's Wall isn't particularly remarkable, but the sections of wall to both the east and west are marvellous and have some fine views of the surrounding countryside. On the 500-metre stretch to the west (along to Thorny Doors, which is a gateway in the wall) you'll find good views north over the farmland (shown below), west down Cawfield Crags and east along the wall over Turret 41A. The section to the east of Caw Gap is much steeper, as the wall climbs up towards Winshield Crags, but after only 250 metres you're rewarded with a great view back down the wall over a dip called Bogle Hole.

» How to get there

A minor road runs right through Caw Gap and there's space on the brow of the hill for one car to park on the roadside. To get to it, take the turning on the B6318 1¾ miles west of Once Brewed, signed "Edges Green, Cawburn". Paths lead both east and west along the wall from here. If the roadside space is occupied you'll have to either walk east from the car park at Cawfields (about 25 minutes – see the previous page for directions) or west from Steel Rigg Car Park (about 35 minutes – see the next page for directions).

» Grid references

NY 727 669 for Caw Gap and roadside parking (nearest postcode NE49 9PH).

44 STEEL RIGG & WINSHIELD CRAGS

If you're short on time, or not up to walking the wall, then the viewpoint at Steel Rigg is a great option. It's right next to a car park and although there isn't an awful lot of foreground the view east towards Peel Crags, Highshield Crags and Crag Lough (a small lake) is very pleasing. If you've got a little bit of time I'd highly recommend Winshield Crags, which is a gentle uphill stroll west along the wall from the car park. After just 10 minutes you get a fantastic view back down to Steel Rigg (pictured above), and it's only another 5 minutes to the trig point on the top, which is the highest point on Hadrian's Wall and has 360° views of the surrounding countryside. Both viewpoints are generally best at sunrise, especially when it's misty.

» How to get there

From the B6318 at Once Brewed, take the turning signposted "Steel Rigg". Follow the road up to the top of the hill where you'll find Steel Rigg Car Park on the right (Pay & Display). Go through the gate at the side of the car park to the viewpoint. For Winshield Crags, turn left out of the car park onto the road, then turn right onto the wall path signed "Caw Gap".

» Grid references

NY 751 677 for Steel Rigg Car Park and viewpoint (postcode NE47 7AW), NY 742 675 for Winshield Crags.

45 PEEL CRAGS

From the eastern end of Peel Crags you get a spectacular view over the remains of Milecastle 39 (also known as Castle Nick). The wall leads the eye nicely towards Crag Lough and Highshield Crags in the background, with Hotbank Crags just visible in the distance. The wall is fairly low at this point, so you can easily lean over to shoot directly along it. It's an ideal location for sunrise, but also in the late evening light.

» How to get there

From the B6318 at Once Brewed, take the turning signposted "Steel Rigg". Follow the road up to the top of the hill where you'll find Steel Rigg Car Park on the right (Pay & Display). Go through the gate at the side of the car park on to the wall path, turn left and follow it along. At the top of the second rise you'll see the milecastle. It takes about 15 minutes and is relatively easy going after the steep first incline. If the car park is full there's space on the roadside halfway up the hill for a couple of cars, and a path beside Peel Bothy onto the wall.

» Grid references

NY 751 677 for Steel Rigg Car Park (postcode NE47 7AW), NY 760 677 for the Castle Nick view.

46 SYCAMORE GAP

Nestled at the bottom of a gap in the crags, right on Hadrian's Wall, is this iconic sycamore tree. The classic shot is from the south side with the crags framing the scene perfectly, but there's plenty of scope for more unusual compositions from the sides. There are a few lichen-covered rocks and tufts of long grass scattered around for foreground, and it's generally more attractive when there are leaves on the tree, so spring through to autumn are the best seasons to visit. The most important thing for a good photo here is to have an interesting sky in the background, whether that's at sunrise, sunset or during the day with moody clouds.

» How to get there

From the B6318 at Once Brewed, take the turning signposted "Steel Rigg". Follow the road up to the top of the hill where you'll find Steel Rigg Car Park on the right (Pay & Display). Go through the gate onto the wall path, turn left and follow it along for about 20 minutes – it's the only tree on this stretch of wall so you can't miss it. If the car park is full there's space on the roadside halfway up the hill for a couple of cars. There's also a lower path on the southern side of the wall, which avoids the ascent and descent of the wall path and is a little bit quicker.

» Grid references

NY 751 677 for Steel Rigg Car Park (postcode NE47 7AW), NY 762 677 for the tree.

access both sides of the wall here to try different angles. The view from the crags looking east over Crag Lough to Hotbanks Farm and Hotbanks Crags is equally impressive (pictured on the right), and there are rocky outcrops and small trees all along the edge for foreground. This view is better in the late evening light when the rock face is lit. There's a sheer unfenced drop on the crag and the best compositions are near the edge, so be very careful in high winds.

47 HIGHSHIELD CRAGS

From the very western end of Highshield Crags you get a fantastic view over Sycamore Gap towards Steel Rigg in the distance (pictured above). The winding wall makes a perfect leading line and it looks superb at sunrise with the warm morning light illuminating the wall, but it's also a great location for sunset as you're looking west. You can also

» How to get there

From the B6318 at Once Brewed, take the turning signposted "Steel Rigg". Follow the road up to the top of the hill where you'll find Steel Rigg Car Park on the right (Pay & Display). Go through the gate at the side of the car park on to the wall path. Turn left and follow it along for about 25 minutes to the crag, which is just after Sycamore Gap. If the car park is full there's space on the roadside halfway up the hill for a couple of cars. Alternatively, you can walk from the layby on the B6318 opposite the Hotbanks Farm access road, which takes about 15 minutes (see the map on page 96 for the exact location). The layby is very narrow and I'd only advise parking here if you're visiting for sunrise or sunset when the road is quiet. There's room for a couple of cars and you need to make sure your car is parked completely off the road (please don't park in front of the farm gates).

Walk along the farm road until you reach a gateway, then go through the gate on the left and follow the footpath up through the woods onto the crags. N.B. it's tempting to explore the eastern shoreline of Crag Lough from here, as there are rowing boats moored just offshore from May through to the end of October, but please note this is private land with no public right of access.

» Grid references

NY 751 677 for Steel Rigg Car Park (postcode NE47 7AW), NY 774 676 for the Hotbanks Farm layby, NY 765 679 for the crags.

48 HOTBANK CRAGS

There are fine views on offer both east and west from these undulating crags. At the western end there's an appealing view down the wall to Crag Lough and the wooded face of Highshield Crags. The wall is quite high at this point though, which makes it tricky to get a strong composition. The wall along the crags is topped with turf all the way along and there's a section in the middle with a double-dip that's particularly attractive (pictured on the right). At the eastern end of the crags you'll find Rapishaw Gap, and the view across this dip with Broomlee Lough and

Sewingshields Crags in the distance is fantastic (pictured above). Since you have a variety of vistas to the east and the west it's suitable from dawn to dusk.

» How to get there

There are three ways to access the crags. If you're visiting during the day I'd recommend parking at Housesteads Fort car park (Pay & Display), which is right beside the B6318, 2¾ miles east of Once Brewed. Go through the visitor centre and follow the wide path out the back up the hill to the fort. When you get to the museum building, walk up the field behind it (aiming for the top left corner) and follow the path to the wall. When you reach the wall, stay on the path next to it. You'll descend from Housesteads Crags, go up onto Cuddy's Crags and descend again at Rapishaw Gap before finally arriving at Hotbank Crags. It takes about 30 minutes and there is a lower path that bypasses Cuddy's Crags. Alternatively, you can make your way up from one of two laybys on the B6318. For the western end of the crags, park in the layby opposite the Hotbanks Farm access road (see the map on page 97 for the exact location). The layby is very narrow and I'd only advise parking here if you're visiting for sunrise or sunset when the road is quiet. There's room for a couple of cars – make sure your car is parked completely off the road and please don't park in front of the farm gates. Walk along the farm road and go through the gate on the right just before the gateway on the main track. Follow the path up onto the crags, which takes about 20 minutes. You'll find another small layby between Hotbanks Farm and Housesteads that fits one or two cars. Go through the gate just to the west of the layby and follow the footpath up the fields to the wall (aim for the ruined lime kiln). This brings you out at Rapishaw Gap and takes about 15 minutes.

» Grid references

NY 794 684 for Housesteads Fort car park (nearest postcode NE47 6NN), NY 774 676 for the Hotbanks Farm layby, NY 783 679 for the other layby, NY 781 686 for Rapishaw Gap, NY 774 684 for the western end.

49 CUDDY'S CRAGS

The view from Cuddy's Crags looking east towards Housesteads Crags is one of the most iconic on Hadrian's Wall (pictured below). The sweeping curve of the grass-topped wall leads the eye through the frame to the small copse of trees perched on the ridge beyond. There's a scattering of rocks for foreground and it's primarily a sunrise location. Also worthy of attention is the view from the other end of the crag, looking west over Rapishaw Gap to Hotbank Crags. Furthermore, on the walk up you'll pass Milecastle 37, which is well preserved and includes an attractive gateway.

» How to get there

Park at Housesteads Fort car park (Pay & Display), which is right beside the B6318, 2¾ miles east of Once Brewed. Go through the visitor centre and follow the wide path out the back up the hill towards the fort. When you get to the museum building, walk up the field behind it (aiming for the top left corner) and follow the path to the wall. When you reach the wall, stay on the path next to it. You'll then descend from Housesteads Crags and Cuddy's Crags is the next hill you come to.

» Grid references

NY 794 684 for Housesteads Fort car park (nearest postcode NE47 6NN), NY 783 687 for Cuddy's Crags.

50 HOUSESTEADS FORT

This is one of the best preserved Roman forts on Hadrian's Wall, and in my opinion the most photogenic. Sitting high up on a ridge the walled complex covers five acres and has wide views over the surrounding farmland. There are various ruined buildings inside, which provide plenty of foreground to combine with the views. The remains of the granary and the communal toilets are particularly interesting, but there's also a fine view looking east over the north gate to the small copse of trees on Kennel Crags (pictured above). The fort is only open during the day, which does limit the photographic potential somewhat, but an interesting sky or conditions such as mist, snow or frost easily make up for this. The lichen-covered stonework also lends itself well to black and white photography. It is a very popular tourist attraction, so I'd advise going early or late to avoid the crowds.

» How to get there

Park at Housesteads Fort Car Park (Pay & Display), which is right beside the B6318, 2¾ miles east of Once Brewed. Go through the visitor centre and follow the path out the back up the hill to the fort. See www.english-heritage.org.uk for ticket prices and opening times (entrance is free for English Heritage and National Trust members).

» Grid references

NY 794 684 for Housesteads Fort car park (nearest postcode NE47 6NN), NY 790 688 for the fort.

Extra Locations

Castles & Countryside

» Blawearie

High up on Bewick Moor are the atmospheric ruins of Blawearie House, which has been derelict since the 1940s. It's guarded by a cluster of mature trees and there's a sandstone outcrop beside it that's splashed with white lichen. Added to this, the surrounding area is covered in a mixture of bracken, heather and long grasses, giving you umpteen angles and different compositions to investigate. Moody skies in any season exaggerate its remote, windswept feel, but visit on a sunny day in late summer and it's an oasis of green among the vibrant purple heather. Not far from the ruins there's also a circular Bronze age burial cairn that's worth a look.

How to get there: From the A697, about 6 miles south of Wooler, take the turning to Alnwick onto the B6346. After 2 miles you'll come to a T-junction. Turn left and continue for 1 mile to Old Bewick – a small collection of buildings on the right, with a red post box on the corner. Park considerately on the verge and walk up the track in front of the cottages. Go through the gate straight in front of you and follow the track all the way to Blawearie. It takes about 30 minutes and after the initial steep section it's a reasonably gentle walk. The cairn is on the left just before the ruins.

Grid refs: NU 067 215 for Old Bewick parking (postcode NE66 4DZ), NU 084 224 for Blawearie.

» Hepburn Moor

On the western edge of Hepburn Moor are Hepburn Crags, which have extensive views across the Chillingham Estate towards the Cheviots in the distance. The top of the crags are strewn with rocks, bracken, heather and small rowan trees, so there's plenty of foreground to choose from to complement the views. There's also a ruined bastle house standing in one of the fields below that makes a good close-up subject. To the northeast of the crags there's an expanse of heather moorland, with an isolated patch of Scots pine trees, and this area looks fabulous in late summer when it's carpeted in purple. If you want to stretch your legs further, moving northeast again is a high point called Ros Castle, with more similar views of the surrounding countryside.

How to get there: The crags are to the southeast of Chillingham Castle. From the castle, drive south and take the left turn to Hepburn. Follow the single-track lane along and through the farm. A minute or so past the farm you'll find a free car park on the right. Take the track out of the back of the car park and about 20 metres past the barrier you'll find a tiny, barely-noticeable path on the left that leads up onto the crags. It's very steep and difficult underfoot, but only takes about 10 minutes. From the crags a path runs across the moor to Ros Castle. If you don't fancy the tricky climb up onto the crags from the car park, continue driving up the road onto the moor and park on the verge where you see a path cross. The path on the right leads to the crags and the path on the left takes you up Ros Castle. (N.B. the road over the moor is single-track nearly all the way to the A1.)

Grid refs: NU 072 248 for the car park (nearest postcode NE66 4EG), NU 074 247 for Hepburn Crags, NU 081 253 for Ros Castle.

›› Fontburn Reservoir

This small reservoir is tucked away to the south of Rothbury and is very popular for fishing. The main attraction for photographers is the pumping tower and "plughole" overspill. This looks superb when shot long-exposure, although you will need a very wide-angle lens to get it all in. The water only overflows when the reservoir is full though, so this location is only suitable during the winter months. It usually starts to overflow in November or December and continues into March if the weather has been very wet.

How to get there: From Rothbury take the B6342 towards Hexham and Cambo. After 6½ miles take the right turn to Fontburn Reservoir, which is on a sharp left bend and signposted with a brown tourist sign. Follow the single-track lane up to the reservoir (there are plenty of passing places) and you'll find a car park at either end of the dam (both free). The overspill is on the left side and you have to shoot from the lane, but there's very little traffic.

Grid ref: NZ 049 936 for the reservoir (nearest postcode NE61 4PL).

›› Hexham Abbey

This beautiful abbey is a must-visit if you're interested in photographing interior architecture. There's been a church of one form or another on this site for over 1300 years, but the current building, which is Early English in style, dates from the 12th century. The outside is very handsome, especially the eastern end as viewed from the market place, but inside is spectacular. There are soaring stone arches, fabulous stained-glass windows and an elegant gallery, with plenty of subjects for details shots too. Entrance is free, although donations towards the upkeep of the building are very welcome. See www.hexham-abbey.org.uk for opening times.

How to get there: From the A69, take the turning at Bridge End roundabout to Hexham onto the A6079. After you cross the bridge, go straight on at the first roundabout, then left at the second roundabout towards the hospital. Follow the road along, past the train station and retail park, and go right at the mini-roundabout at the end. Continue up the street and turn right where you see a statue on a traffic island. The Abbey is just down this road on the left and there's plenty of roadside parking, with more in the market place at the end of the road.

Grid ref: NY 935 641 for the Abbey itself (postcode NE46 3NB)

Other Extras

» Angel of the North

At a towering 20 metres high, with wings stretching 54 metres across, this iconic sculpture is a popular stop-off on the way to Northumberland. Designed by sculptor Antony Gormley and built in 1998 it's made from 200 tonnes of steel. There's unfortunately nothing in the background, so an interesting sky of some kind helps significantly here, although blue skies contrast very well with its appealing rust colour. Sunset is also a great time to visit as its graphic form is silhouetted against the colourful sky. It is a popular visitor attraction though, so getting a clear shot during the day can be problematic, but adding people to the scene does add a sense of scale.

How to get there: The sculpture is on the south side of Gateshead, just off the A1 at junction 66. Follow the signs for Gateshead South onto the A167 and you'll find it on the left. There's a free parking area right next to it. It's open all the time and is free to visit.

Grid ref: NZ 264 578 (nearest postcode NE9 7TY).

» Newcastle and Gateshead Quayside

If the weather in Northumberland isn't cooperating, or you just fancy a night in the city, then I'd highly recommend visiting the quayside along the River Tyne. When the wind is low and the buildings and bridges are reflected in the water there are many fantastic scenes to explore. One of the most photogenic structures is the fabulous curved Millennium Bridge, but the south bank also has some very eyecatching buildings, such as The Baltic art gallery and The Sage (a glass-faced concert venue). The best views are generally from the north bank (i.e. the Newcastle side) and sunset is a great time to visit, as is "blue hour" – the hour after sunset where the sky is a deep blue colour and contrasts wonderfully with the lights. For a higher view, try from the Tyne Bridge or the balcony on Level 4 of The Baltic.

How to get there: There are various car parks near the quayside, such as Sandgate car park in Newcastle (NE1 2NG) or at The Sage in Gateshead (NE8 2BA). Wherever you park, head for the Millennium Bridge for starters. If you don't fancy driving in the city, you can park further out and get the train or metro to Newcastle Central Station or Gateshead Metro Station, both of which are a 15 minute walk to the bridge.

When to Visit

Northumberland has a lot to offer in every season as the coastal locations and those along Hadrian's Wall are superb all year round. Whether you've got moody storm clouds in winter, mist in autumn or a perfect blue sky in summer, there are plenty of places to choose from. Having said that, most of the locations along the coastline are primarily sunrise locations, so many photographers prefer to visit in the winter months when dawn is at a much more manageable hour. However, the weather can be pretty challenging at this time of year, and although it's generally drier than other places in the North, it is colder and does get its fair share of snow.

Autumn and spring offer a good compromise – sunrise is still at a fairly reasonable time of day and the weather is generally better. The countryside also starts to come alive in late spring as fields of bright yellow rapeseed appear all over the county. In autumn the woodlands are bursting with rich colours and mist is a possibility at Hadrian's Wall.

Unsurprisingly Northumberland gets much busier during the summer months, and parking in some places along the coast, such as Embleton Bay and Low Newton-by-the-Sea, can get very tricky. If you're visiting for sunrise or sunset you shouldn't have a problem though. Sea fog can occasionally be a problem on the coast at this time of year, although it does bring added potential for very atmospheric shots, if it's not too thick that is. You can always escape the fog by heading inland to the countryside, which is at its best in summertime. The rolling farmland is a patchwork of greens and golds, with plenty of hay bales scattered in the fields, and in late summer the heather moorlands are awash with vivid purples.

Shooting Seascapes – Practical Advice

Many of the locations on the Northumberland coast can be safely photographed at any state of tide, but there are a few places where you can easily get caught out by rising water levels. I've pointed these out in the location details, but wherever you are always make sure you have an escape route back to the shore. If possible, try to shoot on an outgoing tide, which allows you to focus on your photography rather than worrying about the sea. Occasionally getting wet is part of the fun of shooting seascapes, but getting trapped or falling in while hastily retreating is quite different!

Sea spray can often be a problem on the coast, particularly with a northerly or easterly wind, and can coat your lens in seconds, so make sure you have a good stock of lens cloths or wipes with you at all times. If you have a UV filter, make sure you put it on, as it's a lot easier to clean a filter afterwards than it is the front element of your lens.

Sensible footwear with good grip is a given for clambering over slippery rocks on the coast, but wellies are invaluable at a lot of coastal locations, enabling you to get into the best position without worrying about wet feet. Waterproof trousers also go someway to stopping errant waves going down your wellies. Once home, make sure you clean your lens and camera, and wash your tripod legs with freshwater to prevent corrosion.

If you're shooting long-exposures, make sure your tripod is as sturdy as possible. Place the legs on rocks if you can, but if sand is your only choice and you're in the surf, dig it deep into the sand to prevent movement as the waves wash past. And be careful where you leave your gear – I'm a fan of dumping my rucksack while I wander around looking for compositions, but that can easily end in soaked kit if you're not keeping an eye on the waves.

Tide Times

There are two high tides and two low tides every day, with roughly six hours between each high and low tide. Tide times can be found on many websites, such as www.tidetimes.org.uk, www.tidetimes.co.uk or the BBC weather website. For all the coastal locations in the book I've given the closest tide station and advised whether it's better at low, mid or high tide. The height of the tide can vary significantly with the lunar cycle and the weather though, so you may need to adjust your timings to compensate. Around the new moon and full moon you get spring tides, with higher than average high tides and lower than average low tides. Inbetween spring tides you get neap tides, which have a lower tidal range. High tides are also much higher around the equinoxes (mid March and mid September) and strong winds also create tidal surges, creating higher than usual tides.

Astrophotography & The Northern Lights

Northumberland has some of the darkest night skies in the UK, making it a great place for astrophotography. On a clear night you can see millions of stars and the dazzling arc of the Milky Way. The National Park, along with the Kielder area, is in fact a designated International Dark Sky Park, but you can get great photos from many other places in the county. Bamburgh and Holy Island are both marvellous locations to shoot the night sky from – Bamburgh Lighthouse and the old boats at Holy Island harbour both work really well as foreground interest. Or if you're near Hadrian's Wall, Cawfields Quarry is a superb place to go. If star trails are your aim, the magnificent gatehouse at Dunstanburgh Castle and the tree at Sycamore Gap make perfect focal points. There's also an observatory at Kielder that runs astrophotography events, as well as stargazing evenings (www.kielderobservatory.org).

If you've never done astrophotography before and fancy giving it a go, a wide-angle lens is best. Set it to the widest aperture (e.g. f/2.8) and choose an ISO of 400-1600 (you'll have to experiment with the ISO to find a balance between brightness and acceptable noise on your particular camera). Mount your camera on a sturdy tripod, switch off auto-focus and manually focus on infinity (marked on your lens with the ∞ symbol). Then try exposures of 10-30 seconds (anything over 30 seconds and you'll start to get star trails). If you do want to shoot star trails, things get a lot more technical – the most popular method is to take multiple 30-second exposures over a period of minutes or hours, and combine them in post-processing.

As well as beautiful starry skies, Northumberland is also blessed with occasional displays of the captivating Northern Lights. The best place to get information about the likelihood of sightings is from Aurora Watch, which is run by the University of Lancaster. They issue alerts when the aurora may be visible in the UK and you can get these via email or social media (see their website aurorawatch.lancs.ac.uk for details). You need an amber alert or higher to be in with a chance of seeing it in Northumberland, and of course you need clear skies too. Aurora activity happens all year round but is rendered invisible in the summer months by the light nights, so late autumn through to early spring is the most likely time to see it.

If an alert has been issued, the three best places to head to are St Mary's Lighthouse, Bamburgh and Holy Island. If you can't get to one of those, make your way to anywhere along the coast that's away from light pollution and has a view towards the northern horizon. As for time of night, this wonderful spectacle can occur at any hour, but chances are generally higher between 10pm and midnight.

Sunrise & Sunset Times

To get great shots you need great light, and the best light is around sunrise and sunset. The first hour of light after sunrise is known as 'the golden hour', as is the last hour of light before sunset — during these times the light is warmer and more diffused. It's usually worth staying for a while after sunset too, as you can get backlit clouds. Here are the sunrise and sunset times for Alnwick (everywhere else in Northumberland is within a minute or two of these times):

	Sunrise	Sunset		Sunrise	Sunset
January 1st	8.34	15.46	July 1st	4.29	21.51
January 14th	8.26	16.05	July 14th	4.44	21.41
February 1st	8.00	16.41	August 1st	5.13	21.12
February 14th	7.33	17.09	August 14th	5.38	20.44
March 1st	6.58	17.42	September 1st	6.12	20.00
March 14th	6.25	18.08	September 14th	6.37	19.27
April 1st	6.39	19.44	October 1st	7.09	18.43
April 14th	6.06	20.10	October 14th	7.35	18.10
May 1st	5.26	20.44	November 1st	7.12	16.28
May 14th	4.59	21.08	November 14th	7.38	16.03
June 1st	4.33	21.39	December 1st	8.10	15.41
June 14th	4.25	21.50	December 14th	8.27	15.36

The Sun rises in the east in the morning, and sets in the west in the evening, but there are seasonal variations in the exact direction. The diagram on the next page shows sunrise and sunset directions for different months of the year. To figure out how the light will behave at your chosen location use the diagram in combination with an OS map. There are also a few apps available to help you figure out lighting conditions, such as the Photographer's Ephemeris.

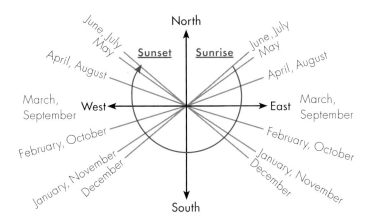

Don't forget that if you've got high ground to the east of you then you won't get direct sunlight on the foreground until well after sunrise (this is particularly true in winter when the Sun doesn't rise as high in the sky). This doesn't mean it's pointless going for sunrise at a location like this, as the Sun may be illuminating something east facing in the background. The same rules apply for sunset with high ground to the west — you'll lose direct light well before sunset, but again if your point of interest in the midground or background is illuminated in beautiful warm light then it's still worth going.

Parking & GPS Coordinates

Most of the recommended parking spots are car parks as Northumberland has plenty along the coast and at the main sights in the countryside. A lot of them are free and those that aren't are generally very reasonably priced (the exceptions being Holy Island and Hadrian's Wall, which are a bit more expensive). Some tickets are transferable to other car parks nearby for the length of time you've paid for (check the parking meters for details).

Using the postcodes given in the book on your satnav often won't take you to the exact parking spot, as many of them aren't near any buildings. If your satnav accepts GPS coordinates you can find a list for all the locations at www.longvalleybooks.com/articles.html and these will take you right to them.

Most of the locations listed are accessible by public transport — visit the local tourist information centre for details of busses and trains. There are a few that have very limited or no public transport links, although they are within a day walk of bus stops, e.g. Simonside and Roughting Linn.

Location Summary Table

Difficulty of walk = * flat and even, **mostly flat but uneven underfoot, *** medium gradient, **** steep gradient.

Photographic interest = * good only in perfect conditions or few surrounding photographic opportunities, **** good in most conditions or lots of different photographic opportunities.

	Location	Type of Location	Difficulty of Walk	Time from car park	Photographic interest
1	Berwick-Upon-Tweed	Various	*	2-8 mins	**
2	Spittal Beach	Beach	*	2 mins	*
3	Cocklawburn Beach	Seascape	**	2 mins	***
4	Lindisfarne Castle	Castle	*	15 mins	****
5	Holy Island Harbour	Harbour	*	8 mins	****
6	Lindisfarne Priory	Priory	*	6 mins	*
7	Emmanuel Head	Views	**	45 mins	*
8	Holy Island Causeway	Views	*	4 mins	***
9	Budle Bay	Views	**	25 mins	**
10	Bamburgh Castle	Castle	*	2 mins	****
11	Beadnell	Harbour	*	4 mins	**
12	Low Newton-by-the-Sea	Harbour & seascape	**	12 mins	**
13	Embleton Bay	Beach	*	3 mins	***
14	Dunstanburgh Castle	Castle	**	15-35 mins	****
15	Black Hole	Seascape	**	15-20 mins	*
16	Cullernose Point	Seascape	**	5 mins	***
17	Howick Scar	Seascape	***	2 mins	***
18	Rumbling Kern	Seascape	**	4 mins	***
19	Sugar Sands	Seascape	**	2-20 mins	**
20	Alnmouth	Various	*	Various	***
21	Amble	Pier	*	4 mins	*

	Location	Type of Location	Difficulty of Walk	Time from car park	Photographic interest
22	Low Hauxley	Seascape	* *	2 mins	* * *
23	Cresswell	Seascape	*	2-8 mins	* *
24	Newbiggin-by-the-Sea	Sculpture	*	2-10 mins	*
25	Cambois Beach	Seascape	*	2 mins	*
26	Blyth	Seascape	*	2 mins	* * * *
27	Seaton Sluice	Seascape	* *	5 mins	* * *
28	St Mary's Lighthouse	Lighthouse	*	2 mins	* * * *
29	Cullercoats	Seascape	*	2-5 mins	*
30	Tynemouth	Various	*	Various	* *
31	Duddo Stone Circle	Stone circle	* *	20 mins	*
32	Roughting Linn	Waterfall	* * *	5 mins	* *
33	Yeavering Bell	Hillfort & views	* * * *	40 mins	* *
34	Alnwick Castle	Castle	*	5 mins	* * *
35	Warkworth Castle	Castle	*	2-6 mins	* *
36	Edlingham	Castle & views	*	2 mins	*
37	Harbottle Hills	Views	* * *	20 mins	* *
38	Simonside	Views	* * *	1 hour	* * *
39	Hareshaw Linn	Waterfall	* * *	5 mins	* * * *
40	Allen Banks	Woodland & river	* *	15 mins	* *
41	Walltown Crags	Wall	* * *	2-20 mins	* * *
42	Cawfields	Wall	*	N/A	* * *
43	Caw Gap	Wall	* *	3-35 mins	* *
44	Steel Rigg & Winshield Crags	Wall	*	2 mins	* *
45	Peel Crags	Wall	* * *	15 mins	* * *
46	Sycamore Gap	Wall	* * *	20 mins	* * *
47	Highshield Crags	Wall	* * *	25 mins	* * * *
48	Hotbank Crags	Wall	* * *	30 mins	* * * *
49	Cuddy's Crag	Wall	* * *	25 mins	* *
50	Housesteads Fort	Fort	* * *	10 mins	*

Acknowledgements

P9 © Rod Hanchard-Goodwin (www.bluefinart.com), p10 © Trevor Weddell, p11 © Tim Gainey / Alamy Stock Photo, p12 © Rod Hanchard-Goodwin (www.bluefinart.com), p13 © Dru Dodd (www.drudodd.com), p14 © Stephen Byard, p15 © John Potter (www.jpotter-landscape-photographer.com), p16 © John Finney (www.johnfinneyphotography.com), p17 © Tim Moore / Alamy Stock Photo, p18 © Bill Ward (www.billwardphotography.co.uk), p19 © Gary Waidson (www.waylandscape.co.uk), p20 © Carmelle Stewart-Hook , p28 © Chris Lishman (www.chrislishman.com), p29 © Jim Gibson (www.gisphotographic.co.uk), p30 © Ross Hoddinott (www.rosshoddinott.co.uk), p31 © John Finney (www.johnfinneyphotography.com), p32 © rjbphotographic, p33 © Calum Gladstone (www.facebook.com/CalumGladstonePhotography), p34 © Stephen Boyd (www.stephenboydphotography.co.uk), p35 © Guy Edwardes (www.guyedwardes.com), p36 © David Taylor (www.davidtaylorphotography.co.uk), p37 © Phil Ure, p38 © Reed Ingram Weir (www.4tog.co.uk), p39 © Dru Dodd (www.drudodd.com), p40 © Calum Gladstone (www.facebook.com/CalumGladstonePhotography), p41 © Stu Patterson, p43 © Darryn Wade (www.darrynwadephotography.com), p44 © Dru Dodd (www.drudodd.com), p54 © Steve Clasper (www.facebook.com/SteveClasperPhotography), p55 © Alistair Bennett, p56 © Steve Clasper (www.facebook.com/SteveClasperPhotography), p57 © David Taylor´ (www.davidtaylorphotography.co.uk), p58 © David Burn, p59 © Mike Ridley (mikeridleyphotography.com), p60 © Alan Howe, p61 © Tom Lowe (www.f22digital.com), p62 © Carmelle Stewart-Hook, p63 © Nick Watson (www.njw-images.co.uk), p65 © Guy Edwardes / Getty Images, p66 © Tom Lowe (www.f22digital.com), p67 © Geoff Love Photography (www.geofflove.co.uk), p68 © Dru Dodd (www.drudodd.com), p69 © Chris Frost (www.chrisfrostphotography.co.uk), p81 © Mark Simpson (www.electriclemonade.co.uk), p82 © E Bowness, p83 © David Taylor (www.davidtaylorphotography.co.uk), p84 © Adam Burton (www.adamburtonphotography.com), p86 © Dru Dodd (www.drudodd.com), p87 © Astrid McGechan (www.astridmcgechan.com), p88 © David Taylor (www.davidtaylorphotography.co.uk), p89 and 90 © Mark Sunderland (www.marksunderland.com), p91 © E Bowness, p92 © Ian Cook, p98 Graeme Peacock / Alamy Stock Photo, p99 © David Taylor (www.davidtaylorphotography.co.uk), p100 © Paul McGreevy, p101 © Roger Clegg (www.northern-horizons.co.uk), p102 © Joan Thirlaway, p103 © David Taylor (www.davidtaylorphotography.co.uk), p104 © Chris Frost (www.chrisfrostphotography.co.uk), p105 © Calum Gladstone (www.facebook.com/CalumGladstonePhotography), p106 © Gerry Adcock / Alamy Stock Photo, p107 © John Bentley (john_arc-images on Flickr), p108 © Joan Thirlaway, p109 © Stuart Lamont (www.stuartlamont.co.uk), p110 © Roger Clegg (www.northern-horizons.co.uk). Contains Ordnance Survey data © Crown Copyright 2017.

Index